北 京 通
BEIJING GUIDE

今日中国出版社

1996·北京

<京>新登字 132 号

责任编辑：艾　杉
翻　　译：宋振峰
美术设计：韩凤泽
审　　定：刘宗仁　黄隽青

图书在版编目（CIP）数据

北京通/今日中国出版社编．—北京：今日中国出版社
1996.3
ISBN7－5072－0847－8

Ⅰ．北… Ⅱ．今… Ⅲ．北京—概况 Ⅳ．K921

中国版本图书馆 CIP 数据核字（96）第 00927 号

北 京 通

＊

今日中国出版社出版
（中国北京百万庄路 24 号）
中国国际图书贸易总公司发行
（中国北京车公庄西路 35 号）
北京邮政信箱 399 号　邮政编码 100044
外文印刷厂印刷
1996 年第 1 版第 1 次印刷
17—CE—3065P
ISBN 7—5072—0847—8/Z·190
03200

目　　录

第一章　来到北京

北京概况

地理位置

北京是中国北方城市。市中心位于北纬 39°56′，东经 116°20′。西北毗邻山西、内蒙古高原，南与华北大平原相接，东近渤海。

地势地貌

北京市总面积 16,807.8 平方公里，其中市区 750 平方公里。西部和北部为连绵不断的群山，分属于太行山山脉和燕山山脉。东南部是缓缓向渤海倾斜的平原。山地占全市面积的 62%。永定河、潮白河、北运河、拒马河、泃河五条河流穿越市区汇入渤海。

北京城区海拔 43.71 米；山峰一般在 1,000 – 1,500 米左右，最高峰灵山 2,303 米，而东南平原的最低处海拔不足 10 米。

气候

北京属温带大陆性季风气候，四季分明，有"四

北京的气候

月份		1	2	3	4	5	6	7	8	9	10	11	12
气温 ℃	平均	-4.6	-2.1	4.7	13.0	19.9	23.6	25.8	24.4	19.1	12.2	4.3	-2.5
	最高	10.7	15.5	22.6	31.1	36.6	38.9	39.6	38.3	32.3	29.3	23.3	13.5
	最低	-22.8	-17.6	-12.5	-2.4	3.7	11.2	16.1	12.3	4.9	-1.4	-11.6	-18.0
降水量(毫米)		2.6	7.7	9.1	22.4	26.1	70.4	196.6	243.5	63.9	21.1	7.9	1.6
风速(米/秒)		2.4	2.7	3.0	3.3	2.8	2.2	1.7	1.6	1.8	2.1	2.2	2.5
四季划分(日/月)		冬季 26/10-31/3			春季 1/4-25/5		夏季 26/5-5/9			秋季 6/9-25/10		冬季 26/10-31/3	
天		157 天			55 天		103 天			50 天		157 天	

宜"之美称,即:春宜花,夏宜风,秋宜月,冬宜雪。对旅游者来说,每年 3-6 月、9-11 月是黄金时期。

春秋可穿轻便衣着(夹衣,羊毛衫),夏季单衣即可。相对中国南方来说,北京冬季寒冷干燥,必须携带羽绒服或棉大衣,以备室外御寒之用。春夏与夏秋之交最好带上雨具。

历史

早在 70 万年前,北京周口店地区就出现了原始人群落"北京人"。北京最初见于记载的名字为"蓟"。公元前 1045 年成为蓟、燕诸侯国的都城。从公元前 221 年秦始皇统一中国到公元 937 年,北京一直是中国北方的重镇和地方政权的都城。公元 938 年,统治中国北方的辽以北京(时称燕京)为陪都;以后,金、元、明、清各代都以此地为首都,前后达 650 多年。1949 年 10 月 1 日中华人民共和国成立,北京成为新中国的首都。

人口与民族

北京人口 1,100 多万,其中市区人口约 600 万,加上每天 300 万以上的流动人口,市区显得拥挤。

中国的 56 个民族,都有成员在北京居住。其中汉族人口最多,占 96.5%,其它 55 个少数民族人口为 30 多万,其中回、满、蒙古族最多。

行政区划分

北京市下辖 10 个区、8 个县,包括:四个城区:东城区、西城区、崇文区、宣武区。四个近郊区:朝阳区、海淀区、丰台区、石景山区。两个远郊区：门头沟区、房山区。八个远郊县：昌平县、顺义县、通县、大兴县、平谷县、怀柔县、密云县、延庆县。

进关须知

签证

外国人：计划来北京的外国人，首先应持有效护照向本人所在国的中华人民共和国大使馆、领事馆或中华人民共和国外交部授权的其他驻外机构提出申请并获得签证。

台湾同胞：中华人民共和国外交部驻香港签证办事处和香港中国旅行社两个机构负责办理台胞来大陆的签证。

台胞如绕道美国、日本或其他国家来北京，可在中华人民共和国驻当地的大使馆或领事馆办理签证。

港澳同胞：港澳同胞回内地旅游、探亲，可凭"港澳同胞回乡证"出境。

华侨：华侨回国可不经申请签证，可凭中华人民共和国主管机关签发的有效护照或其他有效证件出入境。

在华期间要随身携带护照、回乡证等有效证件。下榻旅馆、定购机、车票时必须出具，遇到特殊情况时可免去麻烦。丢失护照要立即向本国驻华使馆或北京公安局外国人出入境管理处报告。电话：5255486

中国公安部授权北京、上海、天津、大连、福州、厦门、西安、桂林、杭州、昆明、广州、深圳、珠海等 13 个城市办理"落地签证"。

海关手续

入境时来宾经填写《旅客行李申报单》，并保存到离境时出示，来宾可带适量的现金以及自用的烟、酒、照相机、收音机、电脑、收录机，出关时除合理消耗外，其余应如数带出。

海关申报单上所列的贵重物品，如摄像机、电脑、黄金及其它贵重物品，离境时必须带出中国，否则将征收进口税。

下列物品禁止携带入境：武器、弹药、爆炸物品、对中国有害的印刷品、胶卷、录音录像带、激光唱盘、烈性毒药及麻醉药物、传染病菌的动植物及食品，同时应注意不可将上述物品及珍稀动植物和文物在未经许可的情况下带出中国。

人民币与外币的兑换

在北京只使用中华人民共和国统一货币，即人民币。人民币的单位是元，辅币是角和分，编写符号是**RMB**。纸币有100元、50元、10元、5元、2元、1元、5角、2角、1角、5分、2分、1分共12种，硬币有1元、5角、1角、5分、2分、1分。1元 = 10角 = 100分。

机场、饭店、旅游商店及中国银行各分行都设有外币兑换处，兑换率由中国外汇管理局统一制定。每个兑换处汇率相同，兑换时填写的外币兑换证明应予保存，在将未用完的人民币兑回外币时还要用它作为证明。

在北京可使用信用卡和旅行支票，它们既可在一些宾馆或指定的餐馆、商店使用,也可到银行或兑换处兑换人民币。目前,国外任何一家银行或金融机构签发的旅行支票(包括台湾银行签发的旅行支票)都可在中国银行及银行点兑现。所有兑换处都是全周营业,时间一般为 8:00 - 19:00,饭馆兑换处营业时间一般为 7:00 - 23:00。

外国驻华航空公司

俄罗斯航空公司
京伦饭店
电话:5002412

埃塞俄比亚航空公司
国贸大厦
电话:5050314

法国航空公司
国贸大厦
电话:5051818

芬兰航空公司
赛特大厦
电话:5127180

全日空
国贸大厦
电话:5050258

英国航空公司
赛特大厦
电话:5124070

日本航空公司
长富宫
电话:5130888

加拿大航空公司
燕莎中心
电话:4637901

大韩航空
国贸大厦
电话:5051047

美国联合航空公司
燕莎中心写字楼 1 层
电话:4631111

港龙航空公司　　　　　　汉莎航空公司
国贸大厦　　　　　　　　燕莎中心
电话:5054343　　　　　　电话:4654488

新加坡航空公司　　　　　瑞士航空公司
国贸大厦　　　　　　　　赛特大厦
电话:5053133　　　　　　电话:5123555

泰国航空公司　　　　　　伊朗航空公司
赛特大厦　　　　　　　　国际大厦
电话:5123881　　　　　　电话:5124940

马来西亚航空公司　　　　波兰航空公司
国贸大厦　　　　　　　　国贸大厦
电话:5052681　　　　　　电话:5007215

澳大利亚航空公司　　　　斯堪的纳维亚航空公司
燕莎中心写字楼 1 层　　　赛特大厦
电话:4674794　　　　　　电话:5120575

航空公司售票处

中国民航和其他航空公司
的订票处在西长安街 15 号

国内机票预订　　　　　　民航西单售票处
电话:6013336　　　　　　电话:6017755

国际航班机票预订　　　　首都机场问讯处
电话:6016667　　　　　　电话:4563604/4563107

饭店机票预定

西苑饭店　　　　　　　　崇文门饭店
电话:8313388 – 150/151　电话:5122211 – 0150

丽都假日饭店　　　　　　东方饭店
电话:4376688 – 1903　　　电话:3014466 – 8008

长城饭店　　　　　　　　华都饭店
电话:5005566 – 2272　　　电话:5001166 – 8196

昆仑饭店　　　　　　　　兆龙饭店
电话:5003388 – 2319　　　电话:5002299

北京香格里拉饭店　　　　日坛宾馆
电话:8412211 – 2839　　　电话:5125588 – 1491

外国驻华使馆

阿富汗伊斯兰国　　　　　阿尔巴尼亚共和国
东直门外大街　　　　　　光华路 28 号
电话:5321582　　　　　　电话:5321120

阿尔及利亚民主人民　　阿根廷共和国
共和国
三里屯路 7 号　　　　　三里屯路东五街 11 号
电话:5321231　　　　　电话:5322090

澳大利亚　　　　　　　奥地利共和国
东直门外大街 15 号　　建国门外秀水南街 5 号
电话:5322331－7　　　电话:5322061

巴林国　　　　　　　　孟加拉共和国
塔园大楼 2－9－1　　　光华路 42 号
电话:5325025　　　　　电话:5322521

比利时　　　　　　　　贝宁共和国
三里屯路 6 号　　　　　光华路 38 号
电话:5321736　　　　　电话:5322741

玻利维亚共和国　　　　巴西联邦共和国
塔园楼 3－1－142　　　光华路 27 号
电话:5324370　　　　　电话:5322881

保加利亚共和国　　　　布隆迪共和国
建国门外秀水北街 4 号　光华路 25 号
电话:5321946　　　　　电话:5322328

柬埔寨
东直门外大街 9 号
电话:5321889

加拿大
三里屯路 10 号
电话:5323536

乍得共和国
光华路 21 号
电话:5321296

哥伦比亚共和国
光华路 34 号
电话:5323377

科特迪瓦共和国
三里屯北小街
电话:5321482

捷克共和国
建国门外日坛路
电话:5321531

丹麦
三里屯东五街 1 号
电话:5322431

喀麦隆共和国
三里屯东五街 7 号
电话:5321828

中非共和国
三里屯东三街 1 号
电话:5321789

智利共和国
三里屯东四街 1 号
电话:5322074

刚果共和国
三里屯东四街 7 号
电话:5321658

古巴
建国门外秀水南街 1 号
电话:5322822

朝鲜民主主义人民共和国
建国门外日坛北路
电话:5321186

埃及共和国
日坛东路 2 号
电话:5321825

赤道几内亚
三里屯东四街 2 号
电话:5323679

匈牙利共和国
东直门外大街 10 号
电话:5321431

法兰西共和国
三里屯东三街 3 号
电话:5321331

德意志联邦共和国
东直门外大街 5 号
电话:5322161 - 65

津巴布韦共和国
三里屯东三街 7 号
电话:5323795

圭亚那合作共和国
建国门外秀水东街 1 号
电话:5321337

伊朗伊斯兰共和国
三里屯东六街 13 号
电话:5322040

埃塞俄比亚共和国
建国门外秀水南街 3 号
电话:5325258

越南社会主义共和国
建国门外光华路 32 号
电话:5321155

加蓬共和国
光华路 36 号
电话:5322810

加纳共和国
三里屯路 8 号
电话:5321319

几内亚共和国
三里屯西六街 2 号
电话:5323649

印度共和国
日坛东路 1 号
电话:5321856

伊拉克共和国
秀水北街 25 号
电话:5323385

爱尔兰共和国
日坛东路 3 号
电话:5322691

以色列国
国贸中心 405 号
电话:5052970 - 72

意大利共和国
三里屯东二街
电话:5322131 - 34

日本国
建国门外日坛路 7 号
电话:5322361

约旦哈希姆王国
三里屯东六街 5 号
电话:5323906

大韩民国
国贸中心 4 层
电话:5053171

肯尼亚共和国
三里屯西六街 4 号
电话:5323381

科威特国
光华路 23 号
电话:5322216

老挝共和国
三里屯东四街 11 号
电话:5321224

黎巴嫩共和国
三里屯东六街 51 号
电话:5321560

利比亚
三里屯东六街 3 号
电话:5323666

卢森堡大公国
内务部街 21 号
电话:5135937

马达加斯加
三里屯东街 3 号
电话:5321353

马来西亚
东直门外大街 13 号
电话:5322531

马里共和国
三里屯东四街 8 号
电话:5321687

马耳他共和国
塔园楼 2 - 1 - 22
电话:5323114

毛里塔尼亚共和国
三里屯东三街 9 号
电话:5321346

墨西哥合众国
三里屯东五街 5 号
电话:5322574

蒙古
建国门外秀水北街 2 号
电话:5321203

摩洛哥王国
三里屯 16 号
电话:5321796

莫桑比克共和国
塔园楼 1 - 7 - 1
电话:5323664

缅甸联邦
东直门外大街 6 号
电话:5321425

尼泊尔王国
三里屯西六街 1 号
电话:5321795

荷兰王国
亮马河南路 4 号
电话:5321131 - 34

新西兰
日坛路东二街 1 号
电话:5322731 - 33

挪威王国
三里屯东一街 1 号
电话:5322261

芬兰共和国
塔园楼 1 - 10 - 1
电话:5321817

巴基斯坦共和国
东直门外大街 1 号
电话:5322504

巴勒斯坦国
三里屯东三街 2 号
电话:5321361

巴布亚新几内亚
塔园楼 2 - 11 - 2
电话:5324312

秘鲁共和国
三里屯楼 2 - 82
电话:5324658

菲律宾共和国
建国门外秀水北街 23 号
电话:5321872

波兰共和国
建国门外日坛路 1 号
电话:5321235

葡萄牙共和国
塔园办公楼 2 - 72
电话:5323497

卡塔尔国
塔园楼 1 - 9 - 2
电话:5322231 - 35

罗马尼亚共和国
日坛路东二街
电话:5323442

俄罗斯联邦
东直门北中街 4 号
电话:5322051

沙特阿拉伯王国
三里屯北小街 1 号
电话:5324825

塞内加尔共和国
建国门外日坛东一街 1 号
电话:5322593

新加坡共和国
建国门外秀水北街 1 号
电话:5323926

索马里共和国
三里屯路 2 号
电话:5321752

斯洛伐克共和国
建国门外日坛路
电话:5321531

西班牙

三里屯路 9 号
电话：5323629

瑞典
东直门外大街 3 号
电话：5323331

瑞士
三里屯东五街 3 号
电话：5322736 - 38

坦桑尼亚联合共和国
三里屯亮马河南路
电话：5321491

多哥共和国
东直门外大街 11 号
电话：5322202

土耳其共和国
三里屯东五街 9 号
电话：5322347

斯里兰卡民主社会主义共
和国
建国门外建华路 3 号
电话：5321861

南斯拉夫联邦共和国
三里屯东六街 1 号
电话：5323516

叙利亚共和国
三里屯东四街 6 号
电话：5321372

泰国
光华里 40 号
电话：5321903

突尼斯共和国
三里屯东街 1 号
电话：5322435 - 36

乌干达共和国
三里屯东街 5 号
电话：5321708

大不列颠及北爱尔兰   乌拉圭共和国
联合王国
光华路 11 号   塔园楼 2－7－2
电话:5321961   电话:5324445

委内瑞拉共和国   美利坚合众国
三里屯路 14 号   建国门外秀水北街 3 号
电话:5321295   电话:5323831

也门共和国   扎伊尔共和国
三里屯东三街   三里屯东五街 6 号
电话:5323394   电话:5321995

赞比亚共和国   希腊
三里屯东四街 5 号   光华路 19 号
电话:5321554   电话:5321317

苏丹共和国   阿曼苏丹国
三里屯东二街 1 号   亮马河南路 6 号
电话:5323715   电话:5323276

第二章　游览北京

城市交通

出租汽车

北京有 5 万多辆出租汽车。在机场、火车站、各宾馆、饭店和旅游地，都有出租汽车昼夜服务。车费按租用行驶里程计算，每公里 1.60 - 2.50 元(在车辆后座两侧挡风玻璃上标明)，以 4 公里为起租价。车顶上有出租汽车(TAXI)标志灯，车内仪表盘上方的监督卡有司机的照片、姓名、单位和电话。黄色小面包出租车，每公里 1 至 1.5 元，10 公里起价。出租汽车均视等人、夜间行驶和空驶里程适当加价。

出租车服务

北京出租汽车公司　　　　　北京市旅游出租汽车公司
电话:8582288　　　　　　　 电话:5158605

首都汽车公司　　　　　　　　北新出租汽车公司
电话:5138893　　　　　　　 电话:8426318

公共电、汽车

　　每辆大型公共汽车的前、后门各有一位售票员招呼乘客,市内公共汽车票价不论路程长短一率5角。6:00－8:00、17:00－18:30为交通高峰时间。

双层公共汽车

　　无人售票的双层公共汽车,为北京街头新添一景。它既可代步又能观览市容,双层公共汽车主要行驶在长安街、前门大街、二环路,可到达天安门广场、亚运村、燕莎友谊商城等游览点和商业区。

小公共汽车

　　优越性介于出租汽车和公共汽车之间。车站间隔大、车速快、不拥挤,还可以按乘客要求灵活停车。小公共汽车一般为中型面包车,顶部和车身上都有标志,一望即知。票价在1至6元之间。

公共汽车

市区公共汽车(5:00－23:00)　　　郊区公共汽车
1路－64路　　　　　　　　　　　301－397路

市区夜间公共汽车(23:15－4:40)　郊区无轨电车
201路－212路　　　　　　　　　401－409路

市区无轨电车　　　　　　　　　城镇公共汽车
101－121路　　　　　　　　　　501－541路
　　　　　　　　　　　　　　　901－912路

地铁

北京地铁有两条线路。环线沿北京站、建国门、东直门、西直门、复兴门环城运行,高峰期每隔 3－4 分钟一列。沿途 18 站,是北京城的主要交通枢纽。

另一条线路从苹果园至西单往返运行,沿途可达白云观、军事博物馆、石景山游乐园和首都钢铁公司等处。

复兴门是两条线路的交点,在此换车不需出站。乘车时要注意看清站台上标明的列车运行方向,以免背道而驰。

地铁出入口是灰色方形水泥建筑,上方有标志灯箱,售票处在进站口,票价一律 5 角。

运营时间:5:00－23:00

自行车

骑自行车是北京多数人使用的代步办法和健身方式。北京拥有 800 多万辆自行车。在北京骑车道路平坦。汽车进不去的小胡同,自行车畅通无阻。骑车还是最浪漫的郊游方式。三五知已结伴而行,去一趟颐和园,从天安门广场出发,一个多小时就到了。

许多主要街道都有自行车专用道路,与机动车道之间设绿化隔离带或铁栏杆。窄的旧街道则在路面划有分道线。几乎到处都有自行车存车处,随处乱放自行车将受到处罚。

一些自行车修理部出租自行车,有的宾馆也有这项服务,一般的办法是交 200－800 元人民币作为押金,每小时收费 4 元左右。

　　赛特购物中心的王师傅自行车出租处出租各类自行车。

　　普通自行车:3 元/小时;

　　　　　　　20 元/天(8 小时)

　　山地/变速车:6 元/小时

　　　　　　　40 元/天(8 小时)

脚踏三轮车

　　坐脚踏三轮车游览北京城更具北京风情。脚踏三轮车在饭店门前或繁华街区都可以找到。尽管收费比较贵,仍是值得一试的趣事。

旅行社和饭店

旅行社

北京中国国际旅行社　　　　中国国际旅行社总社
建国门外大街 28 号　　　　复兴门内大街 103 号
电话:5158562　　　　　　电话:6011122

中国旅行社总社　　　　　　中国青旅集团总公司
东交民巷 8 号　　　　　　　东交民巷乙 23 号
电话:5129933　　　　　　电话:5243388

中国天鹅国际旅游公司　　　中国金桥旅游总公司
朝阳区光华东里甲 18 楼　　地安门西大街 171 号
电话:5081166　　　　　　电话:6015993

中国友好旅行社　　　　　　中国光大旅游公司

白石桥路 3 号
友谊宾馆 2 楼 1 层
电话:8499135

西外大街 135 号
北展宾馆 2 层
电话:8325604

北京海外旅游公司
建国门外大街 28 号
电话:5158844

中信旅游总公司
京城大厦
电话:4660088－8953

北京中国旅行社
建国门外大街 28 号
电话:5158844

北京北辰国际旅游公司
朝阳区安慧里三区 10 号
电话:4910683

北京市旅行社
霞公府街 13 号
电话:5134103

北京市神州旅行社
东直门外新源南路 19 号
电话:4677619

北京青年旅行社
丰台区左定门外玉林里 10 号
电话:3292248

北京新华旅游集团公司
复兴门外复兴路甲 23 号
电话:8214878

中国和平国际旅游公司
朝阳门南大街 14 号
电话:5080516

方舟国际旅游公司
朝阳区枣营路甲 3 号
电话:5011122

北京市华远国际旅游有限公司
德胜门西大街汇通祠
电话:6013355

北京先科旅行社

本社拥有联营大型豪华旅游车,中巴旅游车 12 辆及中档标准客房二百多套,拥有一批业务优秀,气质高雅,开朗活泼的业务导游小姐及管理人才。同时可接待国内外大中型旅游团队、散客及会议。可代办国内各航空公司机票、国际机票及火车票、签证等业务。收费合理,恪守信誉。地址:国家科委专家公寓,电话:90868148。

北京旅游热线投诉电话号码:5130828

是北京市旅游局专为中外旅游宾客提供投诉、咨询服务的专线电话,使用中、英、日三种语言,24 小时昼夜服务。当您在北京的旅游生活中碰到烦恼、遇到困难、感到不满意和需要帮助时,请您拨通北京旅游热线投诉电话。

饭店

北京饭店
东长安街 33 号
电话:5137766

北京希尔顿饭店
东三环北路东方路 1 号
电话:4662288

凯宾斯基饭店
朝阳区亮马桥路 50 号
电话:4653388

中国大饭店
建国门外大街 1 号
电话:5052266

钓鱼台国宾馆
海淀阜成路 2 号
电话:8591188

北京贵宾楼饭店
东长安街 35 号
电话:5137788

长城饭店
朝阳区东环北路 10 号
电话:5005566

京广新世界饭店
朝阳区呼家楼
电话:5018888

昆仑饭店
朝阳区新源南路 2 号
电话:5003388

长富宫饭店
建国门外大街 26 号
电话:5125555

王府饭店
王府井金鱼胡同 8 号
电话:5128899

北京香格里拉饭店
紫竹院路 29 号
电话:8412211

北京港澳中心瑞士酒店
朝阳门北大街 2 号
电话:5012288

新世纪饭店
首体南路 6 号
电话:8492001

国际艺苑皇冠假日饭店
王府井大街 48 号
电话:5133388

粤海皇都酒店
王府井大街 2 号
电话:5136666

北京国都茂盛宾酒店
首都机场南小天竺路
电话:4565588

京伦饭店
建国门外大街 3 号
电话:5002266

首都宾馆
前门东大街 3 号
电话:5129988

华润饭店
朝阳区建国路 35 号
电话:5012233

五洲大酒店
安外北辰东路 8 号
电话:4915588

凯莱大酒店
建国门南大街 2 号
电话:5158855

友谊宾馆贵宾楼
白石桥路 3 号
电话:8498888

北京国际饭店
建国门内大街 9 号
电话:5126688

新大都饭店
车公庄大街 21 号
电话:8319988

北京皇家萨斯大饭店
北三环东路甲 6 号
电话:4663388

国贸饭店
建国门外大街 1 号
电话:5052277

香山饭店
海淀香山公园内
电话:2591155

新万寿宾馆
朝阳区将台西路 8 号
电话:4362288

丽都假日饭店
朝阳区将台路口
电话:4376688

建国饭店
建国门外大街 5 号
电话:5002233

和平宾馆
东城金鱼胡同 3 号
电话:5128833

天伦王朝饭店
王府井大街 50 号
电话:5138888

西苑饭店
海淀区三里河路 1 号
电话:8313388

兆龙饭店
工人体育馆北路 2 号
电话:5002299

中苑宾馆
海淀区高粱桥斜街 18 号
电话:8318888

北京大观园酒店
宣武区南菜园 88 号
电话:3268899

赛特饭店
建国门外大街 22 号
电话:5123388

亮马河大厦
东三环北路 8 号
电话:5016688

渔阳饭店
朝阳区新源西里中街 18 号
电话:4669988

北京展览馆宾馆
西直门外大街 135 号
电话:8316633

亚洲锦江大酒店
工体北路新中西街 8 号
电话:5007788

金朗大酒店
东城区崇内大街 75 号
电话:5132288

城市宾馆
朝阳区工体东路 4 号
电话:5007799

东方饭店
宣武万明路 11 号
电话:3014466

友谊宾馆
白石桥路 3 号
电话:8498888

龙泉宾馆
门头沟水闸北路
电话:9843366

圆山大酒店
德胜门外裕民东里 20 号
电话:2010033

光明饭店
朝阳区亮马桥路
电话:4678822

金都假日饭店
北礼士路 98 号
电话:8322288

回龙观饭店
昌平回龙观
电话:2913931

梅地亚中心
复兴路乙 11 号
电话:8514422

民族饭店
复兴门内大街 51 号
电话:6014466

天坛饭店
崇文区体育馆路 1 号
电话:7012277

保利大厦
东直门南大街 14 号
电话:5001188

华北大酒店
朝阳鼓楼外大街 19 号
电话:2028888

华都饭店
新源南路 8 号
电话:5001166

松鹤大酒店
东城区灯市口大街 88 号
电话:5138822

奥林匹克饭店
海淀区白石桥路 52 号
电话:8316688

百乐饭店
丰台蒲黄榆路 36 号
电话:7612233

牡丹宾馆
海淀花园东路 31 号
电话:2025544

台湾饭店
王府井金鱼胡同 5 号
电话:5136688

裕龙大酒店
海淀区阜成路 40 号
电话:8415588

二十一世纪饭店
朝阳区亮马桥 40 号
电话:4663311

新侨饭店
东交民巷 2 号
电话:5133366

燕山大酒店
海淀路甲 138 号
电话:2563388

越秀大饭店
宣武门东大街 24 号
电话:3014499

燕翔饭店
将台路甲 2 号
电话:4376666

燕京饭店
复兴门外大街 19 号
电话:8536688

前门饭店
永安路 175 号
电话:3016688

崇文门饭店
崇文门西大街 2 号
电话:5122211

北纬饭店
宣武区西经路 13 号
电话:3012266

重庆饭店
朝阳区西坝河光熙门
北里 15 号
电话:4228888

德胜饭店
北三环中路 14 号

电话:2024477

天兆大饭店
朝阳区工体东路 18 号
电话:5080088

光华饭店
东环北路 38 号
电话:5018866

哈德门饭店
崇文门外大街甲 2 号
电话:7012244

华侨饭店
北新桥三条 5 号
电话:4016688

日坛宾馆
朝阳区日坛路 1 号
电话:5125588

三元宾馆
东城东直门外斜街 9 号
电话:4678288

竹园宾馆
西城旧鼓楼小石桥 24 号
电话:4032229

西直门宾馆
西城西内大街 172 号
电话:6014455

珠穆朗玛宾馆
西城鼓楼西大街 149 号
电话:4018822

芙蓉宾馆
朝阳区八里庄
电话:5022921

国安宾馆
朝阳区东大桥关东店北街
电话:5007700

清华园宾馆
海淀成府路 45 号
电话:2573355

国泰饭店
建外永安西里 12 号
电话:5013366

樱花宾馆
朝阳惠新东街 17 号
电话:4229830

惠侨饭店
朝阳区惠新东街 19 号
电话:4214061

紫薇宾馆
石景山路 40 号
电话:8878031

蓟门饭店
海淀区学院路黄亭子
电话:2012211

紫玉饭店
海淀增光路 55 号
电话:8411188

风 景 点

中山公园

是明清两代的社稷坛。始建于 1421 年,面向天安门广场,南门临金水河,背倚后河与故宫隔水相望,东靠午门、端门、天安门。社稷坛及其附属建筑占据全园中部,统称为内坛,四周称为外坛。

社稷坛从前是皇帝祭祀土地之神和五谷之神的地方。"社"的意思是土地。"稷"是高粱,是谷物的代表。坛为方形,以象征大地。坛上按天干地支和八卦的方位铺青、红、白、黑、黄五种不同颜色的天然土壤。在社稷坛北面,是一座精巧的木结构大殿,建于 15 世纪初,原名拜殿,又名祭殿。1925 年,孙中山先生逝世后曾在这里停灵。1928 年改名为中山堂。

公共汽车:1、2、4、5、10、20、57
开放时间:夏季:5:30 - 21:30
　　　　　冬季:7:00 - 19:30

劳动人民文化宫

位于天安门的东侧,原址是太庙,建于明朝永乐18年(1420年),嘉靖23年(1544年)改建。这里是明、清两代皇帝祭祀祖宗的地方。每逢有登基、大婚、摄政、凯旋等大典和年节时,皇帝到这里来祭祀祖先。太庙主要建筑是三进大殿(前殿、中殿、后殿)及配殿。1949年以后,改辟为劳动人民文化宫。

公共汽车:1、2、4、5、10、20、52、57

开放时间:夏季:5:30 - 21:30

冬季:8:00 - 16:00

天坛公园

坐落在北京城南永定门内,是明清帝王祭天和祈谷处,为我国现在规模最大的古代帝王祭祀性建筑群。全坛占地约270公顷,分内坛和外坛。坛墙及祈年殿、圜丘建筑均寓意天圆地方、天帝至上的思想。主殿祈年殿为高约38米的三重檐圆形大殿,内中外层殿柱分别代表四季12个月和12个时辰,大殿耸立于三层汉白玉雕栏高台之上。殿院前神道南端为皇穹宇、圜丘等一组建筑,圜丘是当年冬至日皇帝祭天处。皇穹宇为无梁结构,宇前三音石及围墙回音壁更为祭坛增添了天人感应、皇天对话的神秘气氛。园西侧另一组建筑斋宫,是明清皇帝祭天祈谷前三天斋戒住宿处,四周有回廊160余间,御沟两重。公园内还辟有儿童乐园和月季园、双环亭等景区。全园遍植石柏,苍郁蔽天。

公共汽车:6、15、20、39、43、45、54、60、36、17、25、2、106、110 、116、20

开放时间:夏季:6:00 - 21:00

冬季:6:00 - 20:00

地坛公园

位于东城区。始建于 1530 年,是明清两代皇帝每年夏至日祭祀皇地祇神的场所。主要建筑是祭台,为上下两层石质方形台。现每年春节举办大型庙会。

公共汽车:62、104、108、113、119

开放时间:夏季:6:00 - 21:00

冬季:6:00 - 20:00

景山公园

位于故宫正北面,景山高 43 米,过去为城区最高点。在上面可俯视北京中心城区景色。万春亭南与故宫、天安门、前门、永定门、北与地安门、鼓楼、钟楼同处北京市中轴线上。

公共汽车:101、103、109

开放时间:夏季:5:30 - 21:30

冬季:7:00 - 19:30

北海公园

位于北京市中心,故宫西北,是辽、金、元、明、清五个朝代的皇家御园。北海面积 68 公顷,水面占一半以上,全园布局以琼岛为中心,琼岛之顶白塔耸立,四周殿阁相连,建筑精美,古树参天。白塔建于清顺治八年(1651 年),内藏有喇嘛经卷和衣钵。环湖岸上,游廊、亭、台、殿、阁别致多姿。

公共汽车:103、109、107、111、101、5、13、42

开放时间:夏季:5:30 – 21:30

冬季:7:00 – 19:30

颐和园

颐和园位于北京西北郊,离城约 10 公里。原为金代的行宫,明时改称好山园,清改建为清漪园,1860年被英法联军所毁。1888 年慈禧太后挪用海军经费重建,改名颐和园。慈禧和光绪夏季来此避暑,办理朝政。

颐和园包括万寿山、昆明湖两大部分,全园面积290 万平方米,水面约占四分之三。建筑规模宏大,全园计有各式宫殿园林建筑 3,000 余间。园内布局可分为政治、生活、游览三个区域。政治活动区,以仁寿殿为中心,是慈禧太后和光绪皇帝办理朝事,会见朝臣、使节的地方。生活居住区,以玉澜堂、宜芸馆、乐寿堂为主体,是慈禧、光绪和后妃居住之地。风景游览区,以万寿山前山、后山后湖、昆明湖为主,是全园的主要组成部分。

颐和园是一座在国内外享有盛誉的古典园林。从地形的运用到假山的堆造,布局得宜,浑然一体。以高大的佛香阁为主体,把园外数十里的西山群峰和玉泉山的宝塔都组织到园内画面中来,充满诗情画意。其园林布局,集我国造园之大成。排云殿、佛香阁等一组建筑,雄伟堂皇。长廊沿昆明湖北岸而建,长达 728 米,枋画 14000 多幅,有"画廊"之称。石舫,中西合璧。谐趣园为"园中之园",具有江南庭园风格。

在广阔的湖面上,点缀三个小岛,一道长堤,又以十七孔桥联结东堤,使全园互为呼应。后山后湖,树多景雅,环境幽静。香岩宗印之阁为仿藏式庙宇建筑,造型奇特。苏州街原为宫内的民间买卖街,现已修复。

　　公共汽车:301、303、318、330、332、333、346、374、
　　　　　　375、905
　　开放时间:夏季:6:00 - 19:30
　　　　　　冬季:6:30 - 18:00
电　话:2581144 - 224 或 226

圆明园遗址

　　位于北京西北郊。始建于 1709 年,历时 150 年陆续建成,它是环绕"福海"的圆明、万寿、长寿三园的总称。占地 300 多公顷,为清代皇家宫苑,原有建筑物 145 处,名胜 40 景,艺术价值很高,被誉为"万园之园"。1860 年遭英法联军劫掠焚烧,全园化为废墟,现修整为遗址公园。

　　公共汽车:375、365、331

明十三陵

　　位于北京市北郊 50 公里处军都山南麓。这里埋葬着明代十三个皇帝,目前正式开放供游人参观的有长陵和定陵。长陵是明成祖朱棣墓,是十三陵中规模最大、建得最早的一座。定陵是明万历皇帝朱翊钧墓,是十三陵中发掘最完整的一座,游人可进入地宫,参观地下宫殿和保存在那里的棺椁。另有十三陵路两侧的大宫门、碑亭、石像和龙凤门等景点。

　　公共汽车:前门、崇文门、东大桥、展览路每日有

　　　　　直达旅游车。
　　开放时间:定陵博物馆:夏季:8:30－17:00
　　　　　　　　　　　冬季:8:30－16:30
　　　长陵博物馆:夏季:7:00－19:00
　　　　　　　　　　冬季:8:00－17:30

天安门广场

　　位于北京市中心,面积44公顷,是世界最大的城市广场。广场四周,北有天安门城楼,南有正阳门城楼,西有人民大会堂,东有中国历史博物馆、中国革命博物馆,广场中央是人民英雄纪念碑,碑南是毛主席纪念堂。

　　公共汽车:1、4、10、22、52、57、特1路。

八达岭长城

　　长城始建于公元前七世纪春秋战国时期,用来防御北方异族入侵中原。此后历代对长城修筑使用,是中国古代一项宏大的建筑工程。长城东起山海关,西至嘉峪关,全长6,000公里。古时有关隘,有驻兵戍卫。城墙上有城台、碉堡以及烽火台等供守军使用。长城是北京旅游必去之处,人称"不到长城非好汉"。

　　古都北京城西北方屏障八达岭的长城,是明代长城建筑中独具代表性的地段。在岭口上设有雄伟的关城一座,关城门额题为"北门锁钥"和"居庸外镇"。城墙高大坚固,用花岗岩条石和特制城砖砌筑而成,高约6－7米,顶宽约4－5米,可容五马并骑。墙顶分段设置敌台、垛口和射洞,还特设有排水系统。城墙旁视野开阔处附设古代传递军情信号的烽火台。

为满足旅游观光,近年来在关城附近建设了长城博物馆、秦俑展览及元代军事家成吉思汗行宫。八达岭下有重要关口居庸关、以石雕艺术著称的元代"云台"及关沟的北宋穆桂英点将台,青龙桥火车站有当年京张铁路总设计师詹天佑铜像等名胜古迹。

交通:前门、展览馆、东大桥均有直达旅游车。

慕田峪长城

京东北约 73 公里处的怀柔山区慕田峪长城,西接居庸关,东连古北口,是明代京师长城防御工程的精华地段之一,经大力修复,已于 1988 年正式开放参观。开放参观的 3,000 米长城地段,密集地布局有 15 座敌楼,其中 4 号敌台正关台、三座敌楼并峙,为万里长城各段所罕见;14 号敌台属能藏兵的空心结构,台外存有当年的烽火台。此外,慕田峪长城东南部还有三道长城交汇于一台的奇特景观。慕田峪长城岭谷中林木葱郁,树龄百年以上的古松即达 200 余株,有著名的迎宾松、王冠松、鸳鸯松等。春日山花烂温,秋日红叶满山。游览区兴建有通向 8 号、10 号敌台的登山步道和多种旅游服务设施,以及通向 13 号敌台的登山缆车。近年被评为新北京十六景之一。

交通:每日由东直门发车。

北京动物园

位于西直门外大街 137 号。园内饲养动物有 600 多种,5000 多只,集中了世界上多种珍禽异兽。内有熊猫、金丝猴等世界稀有动物。

公共汽车:107、111、105、7、15、16、19、27、45

开放时间:夏季:6:30－19:00

　　　　　　冬季:7:00－17:00

香山公园

　　位于北京市西北郊。香山最高峰——妙庐峰海拔577米。香山秋有满山红叶,冬有"西山睛雪",春夏有茂林密荫,四季景色迷人,公园设有通往山顶的直达缆车。

　　公共汽车:318、333、360

　　开放时间:夏季:7:00－18:00

　　　　　　冬季:8:30－17:00

八大处公园

　　位于北京市西山,离市中心约25公里,面积3000公顷。山中自隋唐至明清依山修建有八处寺庙,称为八大处。有"三山八刹十二景"之称。其中二处灵光寺的佛牙舍利塔,供奉有佛祖释加牟尼的佛牙舍利。公园每年9、10月间举行八大处游山会。园内设有缆车直达山顶,并设有自山顶而下、全长1700米、落差为240米的滑道。

　　公共汽车:347、311、389

　　开放时间:夏季:7:00－19:00

　　　　　　冬季:8:00－17:00

大观园

　　坐落在北京城西南隅护城河畔,是再现世界文学名著《红楼梦》小说典型环境的文化名园。中国古典小说家曹雪芹笔下的大观园,是一座"天上人间诸景备,衔山抱水建来精"的大庭院,集我国古代园林建筑艺术之大成。而北京的这座大观园,从园林建筑、山石水系以至园林花卉、小品点缀等,都是力求按照《红楼梦》里的描写,精心设计建造的。全园占地 12.3 万平方米。主要庭园和园景有怡红院、潇湘馆、秋爽斋、稻香村、栊翠庵、省亲别墅牌坊等。园内每天有真人表演,再现当年"红楼梦"中的生活情景。

公共汽车:61 路(原 10 路)

开放时间:8:30-16:30

中华民族园

位于北京市城西。园内建有按 1:1 比例建造的中国苗、藏、彝、侗、布依、朝鲜、傣族等民族村寨,由各族演员在各自的寨子里表演本民族舞蹈或本民族的生产、生活场景。

公共汽车:特专车,西便门发车。

开放时间:8:30-17:30

世界公园

位于城南。占地 46.7 公顷,建有按比例缩小的世界 30 个国家的 106 个著名风景名胜。

专车,西便门发车。

开放时间:8:00-18:00

老北京微缩景观

位于昌平县,内有按比例微缩的 15 世纪时北京的城墙、店铺、胡同、茶馆以及老北京人的生活风貌。

公共汽车:345、动物园前有小公共汽车直达

开放时间:9:00-17:00

明皇蜡像宫

位于十三陵旅游风景区,由明皇蜡像宫、仿明乐舞宫、明膳宫、明皇宫购物中心和多功能厅组成。蜡像宫再现了明朝皇宫朝廷日常风貌。

公共汽车:345、动物园前有小公共汽车直达。

开放时间:9:00 – 17:00

陶然亭

位于永定门外太平街 19 号,已有 500 多年的历史。园内有湖,湖中有岛, 还有各式各样风格迥异的亭、阁。

公共汽车:102、59、14

开放时间:夏季:5:30 – 21:30

　　　　　冬季:7:00 – 19:30

鼓楼,钟楼

位于地安门外大街。鼓楼建于元 9 年(1272 年)。鼓楼是古代报时的地方,原设有定时的"铜漏壶"和定更的更鼓。

钟楼在鼓楼的北面,是明永乐年间所建,楼上有一口大铜钟。

公共汽车:107、8

开放时间:8:30 – 16:00

卢沟桥

位于城西南,已有 800 年的历史,因横跨卢沟河而得名。是北京现存最古老的一座石造拱桥,桥身由白石建成,全长 266.5 米,宽 7.5 米,有 11 个桥拱,两旁石栏雕柱各 140 根,柱头上均雕有石狮,共 485 只。

卢沟桥是中国抗日战争爆发地,现建有中国人民抗日战争纪念馆。

公共汽车:309、339

周口店"北京人"遗址

位于北京房山周口店村的北京猿人遗址,为发掘北京猿人头盖骨化石所在地,设有北京猿人展览馆。北京猿人遗址是中国旧石器时代的重要遗址,是研究人类起源、进化的重要科学基地,也是研究中国古脊椎动物学和古人类学的发祥地。

公共汽车:309、339

中央电视塔

位于城西三环路西。高 405 米,为市区最高建筑,在塔楼内了望厅和露天平台可俯瞰北京市区风光。

公共汽车:323、374

北京植物园

位于北京市西北郊。建于 1957 年,占地 300 多公顷,是集植物科研、观赏于一身的园林,有名贵树木近千种,内有竹院、牡丹园、丁香蔷薇园、热带植物园等。

公共汽车:318、333、360

开放时间:8:30 - 16:00

龙潭湖公园

位于城区东南。建于 1952 年,面积约 120 公顷,是一座突出龙文化特色的公园。园内水域广阔,分为东、中、西三湖。园内分为龙潭、龙吟阁、龙门等景区,此外还有龙亭、龙脊桥、"龙"字碑林。

公共汽车:12、41、64

开放时间:8:00 - 17:00

大钟寺

位于城区北三环北侧,又称中国古钟博物馆。以寺内的大铜钟而闻名,有"中国钟王"之美称。大钟铸于明永乐年间,距今有 500 多年历史,钟高 6.94 米,外径 3.30 米,钟唇厚 18.5 厘米,重量 46.5 吨。钟身内外铭有佛教经典 17 种,总计 227,000 多字。钟声宏亮,可传出数公里。每年春节初一到初三,每天早、午、晚撞钟三次。除大钟以外,寺内还收集陈列有历代大小不一的古铜钟 600 多口。

公共汽车:302、367

开放时间:8:30 - 17:30

国子监

国子监创建于元朝大德十年(1306 年),是元明清三代的国家最高学府。占地广阔,有三进院落。辟雍系国子监的中心建筑,是皇帝来国子监讲学的地方。彝伦堂是国子监藏书之所。

公共汽车:13、116、2、18、104、108

开放时间:8:30 - 16:00

博物馆和艺术馆

北京拥有各类博物馆 83 个,为中国之最,博物馆一般开放时间为 9:00 - 16:00,星期一休息。

故宫博物院

坐落于北京城区中心,旧称紫禁城,是中国明清王朝的皇宫,我国现存最大最完整的古代帝王宫殿群。明永乐四年至十八年(1406 - 1420 年)营建,迄今已有 500 多年历史。占地 72 万多平方米,拥有殿宇宫室 9000 余间。宫城建筑壁垒森严,四周是 10 米高墙,50 多米宽的护城河。故宫是明清封建皇权统治中心。建筑布局有内廷与外朝之分。外朝以太和、中和、保和三大殿为轴心,文华、武英二殿为两翼,是皇帝行使权力、登极庆典和召见大臣的主要场所。其中太和殿俗称金銮殿,是故宫最富丽堂皇的建筑,峙立于三层汉白玉雕栏高台上,有 86 根直径 1 米多的楠木擎天柱,殿顶金龙藻井,内设金龙宝座,它是封建皇权至高无上的象征。故宫内廷有与外朝三大殿同在一条中轴线上的乾清宫、交泰殿、坤宁宫和御花园、东六宫、西六宫等,通称三宫六院,是明清帝王处理日常政务的庭院,也是帝王后妃和皇子们居住、玩乐、奉神的地方。故宫内保存有大量珍贵的历史文物,现为全国最大的博物院,近年已列入世界文化遗产清单。

地址:景山前街 4 号

电话:5132255

中国历史博物馆

中国历史博物馆是搜集、收藏中国古代、近代历史文化的机构;又是进行历史科学和有关学术问题研究的机构。收藏文物 6 万余件。《中国通史陈列》是该馆的基本陈列。

地址:天安门广场东侧

电话:5128986

中国革命博物馆

收藏中国自"五四"运动和中国共产党成立以来的革命文物和党史资料,宣传中国共产党的历史,进行革命传统教育的机构。中国革命博物馆 1961 年正式开放,现有藏品近 12 万件,基本陈列有"中国共产党党史陈列(民主革命时期)"。

地址:天安门广场东侧

中国人民革命军事博物馆

1959 年 8 月建成,有第二次国内革命战争馆、抗日战争馆、第三次国内革命战争馆、保卫社会主义革命和建设馆。

地址:海淀区复兴路 9 号

电话:8514441

中国人民抗日战争纪念馆

1987 年创建。位于古老的宛平城内,出城西门即闻名中外的卢沟桥。该馆以图片为主,并配以珍贵实物,反映了"九. 一八"事变至抗日战争胜利这一历程中的重大历史事件。"卢沟桥事变"半景画馆,以逼真的声像效果,使观众犹如身临其境,重温 50 多年前那段沉重、悲壮的历史。

　　地址:丰台宛平城内大街

　　电话:3813163

毛主席纪念堂

　　建成于 1977 年 8 月。中国人民伟大领袖毛泽东的遗体停放在纪念堂的中心——瞻仰厅。在纪念堂内设毛泽东、周恩来、刘少奇、朱德革命业绩纪念室。

　　地址:天安门广场

　　电话:5132277

首都博物馆

　　坐落在东城区幽静的国子监街孔庙内。收藏有新石器时代、以及元、明、清各代的珍贵文物、标本等 8 万余件。基本陈列为"北京简史陈列"。该馆举办的"春节孔庙文化庙会"已成为首都五大特色庙会之一;"国学祭孔乐舞表演"也是该馆举办的具有民族特色的活动。

　　地址:东城国子监街 13 号

　　电话:4012118(星期一休息)

北京自然博物馆

　　建于 1958 年,是一个以反映自然历史为主要内容的博物馆。通过植物、动物、古动物和人类等发展史的陈列,介绍生物科学知识和自然科学知识。馆中巨大的恐龙标本每天都吸引着大量少年儿童。

　　地址:天桥南大街 126 号

电话:754431(星期一休息)

地质博物馆

开放于 1858 年 10 月,主要收藏国内外各类地质标本,设有矿产资源室、地球史室、地层古生物室、矿物岩石室、中国矿床室、宝石室等,是介绍地质矿产、普及地质科学知识、进行地质国际交往的重要场所。

地址:西四南大街羊肉胡同 15 号

电话:6036422

中国体育博物馆

1990 年 9 月 22 日开馆,是我国第一座综合性体育博物馆。其基本陈列是"中国体育展览",包括古代体育、近代体育、新中国体育成就和民族传统体育四个部分。

地址:安定路甲 3 号

电话:4912164

中国美术馆

全馆有大小展厅 14 个,还设有专供美术家进行创作和观摩作品用的画室和艺术交流厅。藏有我国近现代美术杰作数万件、中国民间美术作品 4 万余件。

地址:五四大街 1 号

电话:4012252

北京天文馆

1957 年建成,是普及天文知识场所。馆内设有天象厅、展览厅、讲演厅、天文台和色球台。天象厅也叫星空放映室,中心装有一架中国自制的天象仪,可用来模拟自然星空。色球台内装有色球望远镜,用来观察太阳色球。

地址:西直门外大街138号

电话:8353003(星期五休息)

中国工艺美术馆

是收藏、展览中国工艺美术品的大型美术馆。珍宝馆收藏当代中国工艺美术精品近500件(套),四个陈列室分为陶瓷类、金属雕漆类、织绣类、雕刻类。

地址:复兴门立交桥东北

电话:6013377

石刻艺术博物馆

位于真觉寺金刚宝座塔。是中国第一座按石刻学分类的综合性露天博物馆。藏有6,000多件各类石刻。以金刚宝座塔为中心,分为石刻综合、功德碑、墓志铭、书法碑帖、寺庙碑、会馆碑、石雕7个陈列区。

地址:海淀区五塔寺村24号

电话:8312696

炎黄艺术馆

馆藏品以著名画家黄胄的作品及黄胄先生收藏的历代著名书画家的优秀作品、文物资料为主,兼藏有海内外书画家为该馆捐赠的作品及其和文物资料。该馆还开展对国画及中国传统艺术的研究工作,是一处兼容展览、交流、研习中国书画艺术的场所。

地址:亚运村惠中路

电话:4912902

大葆台西汉墓博物馆

是一座工程浩大的纯木结构的地下宫殿,汉墓的主人是西汉的皇子。陈列室中除了各种珍贵的汉宫饰品以外,还有当年汉武帝实行盐铁官营经济政策的实物见证——"渔阳铁斧",有世界最早的炼钢技术"铸铁脱碳钢"的产品,还有 2000 年前粮食作物和果品的标本。

地址:丰台区郭公庄南

电话:3816688(星期一休息)

名人故居

鲁迅博物馆

1956 年建成开放。位于鲁迅故居东侧。展览大厅根据鲁迅一生活动的时序和地点,陈列着有关鲁迅的文稿、照片、书刊、美术品和其它实物。

地址:阜城门内大街

电话:6021604(星期天休息)

徐悲鸿纪念馆

馆内陈列着徐悲鸿在各个时期的代表作,其中有画家早期在法国的习作,及巨幅油画《田横五百士》和《溪我后》等。展览还以大量的照片和实物介绍了画家的生平活动。

地址:新街口北大街 53 号

电话:2252042(星期一休息)

曹雪芹纪念馆

位于香山正白旗曹雪芹故居内,史家认为小说《红楼梦》就诞生在这里。纪念馆展出曹雪芹当年的起居室;写作《红楼梦》时的书斋;香山地区的地理、自然环境模型;与有关曹雪芹身世的重大发现的实物及资料。

地址:香山正白旗 39 号

电话:2592561 转 370

双清别墅

位于香山公园内,是一座依山而建的庭院,院内有清泉,泉旁石崖上乾隆题"双清"二字。1949 年三月中共中央由河北西柏坡迁至双清,毛主席曾在此居住,庭内展览展出大量资料和照片,记录了毛主席在这里工作和生活的情况。

梅兰芳纪念馆

1986 年 10 月 27 日,梅兰芳 92 岁诞辰纪念日,建成开放。第一陈列室主要以图片和实物介绍梅兰芳生平;第二陈列室为不定期更换展品的专题陈列室;第三陈列室为纪念品、礼品陈列室;故居陈列室是梅兰芳晚年生活的房间,梅兰芳在这里度过了他生命中的最后十年。

地址:护国寺街 9 号(星期一休息)

宋庆龄故居

原是清朝末代皇帝溥仪的父亲醇亲王载沣的府邸——摄政王府花园。中国前国家名誉主席宋庆龄自 1963 年迁居于此,直至 1981 年逝世。故居中展出近 400 幅历史照片和 300 多件珍贵文物资料,展现了宋庆龄不平凡的一生。

地址:西城区后海北岸 46 号

电话:4035858(星期一、四休息)

郭沫若故居

郭沫若从 1963 年至 1978 年逝世,在这里工作生活了 15 年。郭沫若在这里写了数以百万字的论文、专著及诗歌等作品,故居里保存着他遗留下来的大量手稿、图书和文献资料。

地址:西城区前海西街

电话:6022438(星期五休息)

茅盾故居

茅盾在这里度过了他生命的最后 6 年。陈列室里展出了茅盾从童年到逝世各个历史时期的照片近 200 幅,手稿、书籍文献资料、珍贵遗物等 400 多件。

地址:交道口后圆恩寺

电话:4040520

其它博物馆和艺术馆

北京艺术博物馆
海淀区苏州街万寿寺
电话:8413379

民族文化宫
复兴门内大街
电话:6024433
(星期天休息)

大钟寺古钟博物馆

农业展览馆

海淀北三环西路北侧
电话:2550843

东三环北路
电话:5018877

周口店北京猿人遗址博物馆
北京西南周口店
电话:9301404

古观象台
建国门内
电话:5128923
(星期二休息)

北京国际艺苑美术馆
皇冠假日饭店
电话:5133388 转 1209

北京蜡像馆
安定门外地坛公园
电话:4214456
(星期天休息)

北京航空博物馆
昌平县大汤山
电话:2912457

中国科技馆
北三环中轴路 1 号
电话:4221177 转 2211

中国邮票博物馆
宣武门东大街 2 号
电话:3022082

郊野风光

上方山云水洞

　　上方山在北京西南 70 公里处的房山区内,山中有 9 洞、12 峰,早在 1900 多年前东汉时期,这里就建有寺庙。现有公路直到山底,登山有两条路,一条从圣水峪上山;另一条从开凿于 500 年前的"天梯"上山。山上有不少名胜古迹,风景秀美。

云水洞,洞长 620 米,是北方最大的溶洞,洞中有 6 个自然形成的大厅,平均高约 6 米,点缀着千奇百怪的钟乳石,最高者为 37 米。

交通:永定门火车站乘车,房山古山口站下车。

十渡

位于北京西北房山区内 90 公里处,一条河流曲折流经山区,形成 10 个"之"字型的河道,由此得名"十渡",这里的山和水极富特色,似中国桂林的漓江风光,美景如画,有"小桂林"之称。

交通:永定门火车站乘火车,十渡站下车,或莲花池长途汽车站乘旅游汽车。

石花洞

位于北京西南 100 公里处,分为互相连接的 6 层,已经开发的两层长约 122 米,两层垂直距离 40 米。洞中有各种各样的钟乳石,形如猴子、狮子、孔雀等。

交通:夏季前门有旅游车直达。

金海湖公园

位于城东北平谷县境内,距市区 90 公里,这里山清水秀,水域广阔,有划船、水上跳伞、游泳、钓鱼等多种游乐项目。

交通:东直门乘长途汽车。

京东大峡谷

位于城东北平谷县内,全长 6 公里,峡谷内山高崖险,有五大龙潭和天然瀑布。

交通:东直门乘长途汽车到平谷县,再换乘去京东大峡谷的汽车。

湖洞水自然风景区

位于城东北平谷县境内,在一个长约 10 公里的大峡谷中,总面积 9 平方公里,景区里多山、水、湖泊,茂密的森林中是鸟的天然乐园。

交通:东直门乘长途汽车到平谷县,再换乘去湖洞水的汽车。

白龙潭

在城东北密云县,以 3 个相互连接的瀑布著名,水潭位于两山之间,山上森林密布并有奇形怪状的岩石,西面是密云自然保护区。北郊新建有渡假村、游泳池、狩猎场。这里还留有宋朝和元朝时的寺庙。

密云水库

位于城东北密云县境内,面积 188 平方公里,库容 43.75 亿立方米,是北京的主要水源。环水库设有渡假村和数处旅游景点。

交通:东直门乘长途汽车。

云岫谷自然风景区

位于城东北密云县新城子乡,峡谷长 3 公里,谷内有三块大岩石,是第四冰川纪留下的遗迹。谷内有大片的天然分散猴桃园,附近有密云狩猎场。

交通:东直门乘长途汽车。

龙庆峡

位于城西北延庆县境内,距市区 85 公里,峡谷长 7 公里,自然景色迷人,兼有江南景色和北方山水风格。是北京最好的风景区之一。

交通:北郊市场乘旅游车。

康西草原

位于城西北延庆县境内,距市区约 80 公里,面积约 2000 公顷草原。设有跑马场、垂钓区、渡假村。

交通:西直门火车站乘车康庄站下车。

雁栖湖

位于城北怀柔县境内,距市区 55 公里,是雁栖河上的一座人工湖泊。水面开阔,现已建成为水上游乐园。有龙舟、快艇、水上游乐飞机、水上滑梯等项目,设有人工沙滩,可游泳、日光浴,湖岸设有供游人过夜的小木屋。雁栖湖北面是慕田峪长城和云蒙山自然保护区。

宗教圣地

孔庙

孔庙位于安定门内国子监街,创建于元朝大德六年(1302 年)。其规模仅次于山东曲阜孔庙,门内有院落三进。大成殿是孔庙的主要建筑,为祭孔的正殿。

崇圣祠,是祭祀孔子祖先的地方。进士题名碑198方,是研究历代科举制度的珍贵资料。庙内古柏参天,环境幽雅。

公共汽车:13、116、2、18、104、108路。

开放时间:8:30－16:00

雍和宫

位于城区东北角,是著名的喇嘛庙,建于清代康熙33年(1694年)。原为清雍正皇帝的行宫,乾隆9年(1744年)改建喇嘛庙,内中建筑兼含汉、满、蒙、藏风格。这里每旬一日,都举行法会,每年农历正月三十和二月初一都要进行"打鬼"活动。

公共汽车:116、13、44路及地铁。

开放时间:8:30－16:00

天主教南堂

位于城区宣武门,是北京最古老的天主教堂。清顺治七年(1650年),天主教耶稣会教士、德意志人汤若望,在意大利传教士利玛窦所建的经堂旧址上兴建的。教堂内装饰华丽堂皇,每日早晨6:30和星期日上午举行弥撒。

公共汽车:15、25、44、45、48、49、102、105、109路。

在北京的天主教堂还有:西什库的北堂(救世主堂),王府井八面槽的东堂(圣若瑟堂),幸福大街永生巷的南岗子堂(小德肋撒堂),西四南大街57号缸瓦市堂。基督教堂有崇文的晓顺胡同崇文门堂,海淀泄水湖的海淀堂,均有宗教活动。

牛街清真寺

北京有近 18 万人信仰伊斯兰教,对外开放的清真寺有 40 多座。较大的有位于广安门内的牛街清真寺,是北京历史较久、规模较大的清真寺,初建于公元 996 年,1980 年进行大修,全寺建筑既有中国古代建筑形式,又有阿拉伯的建筑风格和伊斯兰的装饰风格。

公共汽车:61、10 路。

东四清真寺

位于东四南大街的东四清真寺内有多种版本的《古兰经》。其中有元代手抄本一部,字体工整,完好无损。中国伊斯兰教协会设于此。

公共汽车:101、119、110、112、116 路。

白云观

坐落于城区西便门外,是北京最大的道观,也是北方道教中心,白云观创建于唐开元年间(713 年 - 714 年)。道教是中国固有的东方宗教,东汉顺帝时(公元 126 - 144 年)张道陵创建此教,奉老子为教祖,认为道无所不包,无所不在,以老子的《道德经》为主要经典。中国道教协会设于此。

公共汽车:19、40、48、49、309 路。

开放时间:9:00 - 16:00

广济寺

广济寺在西四阜成门内大街东口,初建于 800 多年前的金代,这里属金中都的西北郊,名叫西刘村。

以后经过多次重修,现存建筑是明成化年间重修的,
已有 500 多年的历史。近 30 多年来也作过两次修
缮。

寺里有四重殿。第一进是天王殿,左右两侧有
钟、鼓楼。第二进为大雄宝殿,内有三世佛塑像。穿
过一道庭院,后面是圆通宝殿,内有 11 尊观音铜像,
故又名观音殿。最后一进叫藏经阁,又名舍利阁或多
宝殿,殿内陈列有各国佛教人士赠送的礼品。楼上珍
藏明代刻印的大藏经和古代佛教绘画。西路有戒坛,
为汉白玉石筑成,高 3 层。

中国佛教协会就设在寺里。寺内设有图书馆,藏
书 10 多万册。

公共汽车:13、22、47、101、102、103、105 路。

开放时间:9:00 - 17:00

卧佛寺

位于市西北郊香山东侧,距市区 30 公里。卧佛
寺最早创建于唐代贞观年间(公元 627 - 650 年),内
有一尊巨大的铜卧佛,卧佛寺由此得名。卧佛身长 5.
2 米,用铜 250 吨,铸佛用工达 7000 人。铜佛侧身躺
在木榻上,左手平放在腿上,右手弯曲枕着头部,卧
佛周围环立 12 个小佛,据说意为释伽牟尼在菩提树
下临终时,向 12 弟子嘱咐事情的情景。寺内植有菩
提树。

公共汽车:360、333 路。

开放时间:8:30 - 17:00

碧云寺

位于市西北郊香山东麓,初建于元代(1366 年)。依山势而建,从山门到寺院,建筑物逐渐上升,直到山顶。皇帝和妃子们喜爱碧云寺的优美风景,常到此游玩。寺内有罗汉堂,系仿杭州静慈寺所建,内有 500 尊罗汉坐像,其大小和普通人相似。1925 年孙中山先生在北京逝世后,曾在寺内后殿停灵,以后此殿改为中山纪念堂。

公共汽车:360、333 路。

开放时间:8:30 – 17:00

潭柘寺

位于北京西郊门头沟区潭柘山山腰,距市区 40 多公里。初建于晋代(265 – 316 年),是北京地区最古老的一座寺庙,因山上有龙潭、柘树,由此得名潭柘寺。潭柘寺依山势建造,各组殿堂依地形高低错落有序,与周围的山水树木融为一体。寺前有上下塔院,有金、元、明、清各代墓塔数十座,是历代有名的方丈及禅师的墓地。

汽车:展览路乘长途汽车。

开放时间:8:00 – 17:00

戒台寺

位于北京西郊马鞍山上,距市区 35 公里。寺内有中国寺院里最大的戒台,是佛教寺院向信徒传授戒律的地方。戒台寺始建于唐代,现存戒台为明代建造,成正方形,每边 10 米,高 3.5 米。戒台寺以古松多而奇著称。

公共汽车:展览路乘长途汽车。

开放时间:8:00－17:00

法海寺

位于城西石景山区模式口村北,翠微山南麓,明正统四年(1439年)创建。法海寺内存有中国现存最完好的明代壁画,历经500多年,画的色彩仍很鲜明,壁画内容为宗教神话人物。

公共汽车:331、336路。

开放时间:8:00－17:00

第三章　生活在北京

邮政通信

市内电话：在北京，酒店、公共场所、街道等均设有公用电话，可打市区电话。

国际电话：可使用国际直拨电话 IDD 与国外进行电话联系。使用方法为：按顺序将国际冠字(00)、国家代码、城市代码及受话号码连续拨完。如拨打日本东京某电话××××－××××，拨叫方法为：

00 ＋ 81 ＋ 3 ＋ ××××——××××

(国际冠字)(国家代码)(城市代码)(受话号码)

酒店各房间都有国际直拨电话，并有使用方法介绍。

部分国家和地区的国际直拨电话代码

国家和地区	代　码	时　差
中　国	86	
香　港	852	0

澳　门	853	0
台　湾	886	0
朝　鲜	850	+ 1.00
韩　国	82	+ 1.00
印　度	91	− 2.30
印度尼西亚	62	− 0.30
菲律宾	63	0
日　本	81	+ 1.00
伊　朗	98	− 4.30
沙　特	966	− 5.00
土耳其	90	− 6.00
新西兰	64	+ 4.00
澳大利亚	61	+ 2.00
埃　及	20	− 6.00
苏　丹	249	− 6.00
阿尔及利亚	213	− 8.00
坦桑尼亚	255	− 5.00
赞比亚	260	− 6.00
墨西哥	52	− 15.00
古　巴	53	− 13.00
巴　西	55	− 11.00
智　利	56	− 12.00
阿根廷	54	− 11.00
加拿大	1	− 13.00
巴基斯坦	92	− 2.30
孟加拉	880	− 2.00
斯里兰卡	94	− 2.30
缅　甸	95	− 1.30

泰　国	66	−1.00
新加坡	65	−0.30
马来西亚	60	−0.30
美　国	1	−13.00
英　国	44	−8.00
法　国	33	−8.00
德　国	49	−7.00
意大利	39	−7.00
西班牙	34	−8.00
葡萄牙	351	−8.00
瑞　典	46	−7.00
瑞　士	41	−7.00
挪　威	47	−7.00
荷　兰	31	−7.00
希　腊	30	−6.00
俄罗斯	7	−5.00
保加利亚	359	−6.00
捷　克	42	−7.00
南斯拉夫	38	−7.00
罗马尼亚	40	−6.00
波　兰	48	−7.00
匈牙利	36	−7.00

国内电话:在北京可使用长途自动电话直拨国内 2000多个城市和地区,使用方法为:依序将国内冠字 (0)、城市区号、受话号码连续拨完。如拨打上海市 电话2345678,拨号顺序如下:0212345678。各酒店均 备有国内长途自动电话(DDD)国内部分城市长途直

拨电话区号(表)176查询。

国内长途直拨电话城市区号表

通达地点	长途区号	通达地点	长途区号
北京市	10	福建省	
上海市	21	福　州	591
天津市	22	厦　门	592
河北省		泉　州	595
石家庄	311	漳　州	596
保　定	312	武夷山	599
张家口	313	江西省	
承　德	314	南　昌	791
唐　山	315	九　江	792
秦皇岛	335	庐　山	792
邯　郸	310	景德镇	798
山西省		井冈山	7060
太　原	351	山东省	
大　同	352	济　南	531
长　治	355	青　岛	532
临　汾	357	淄　博	533
运　城	359	德　州	534
内蒙古自治区		烟　台	535
呼和浩特	471	潍　坊	536
包　头	472	泰　安	538

通达地点	长途区号	通达地点	长途区号
曲　阜	5473	锦　州	417
河南省		营　口	417
郑　州	371	**吉林省**	
安　阳	372	长　春	431
开　封	378	吉　林	432
洛　阳	379	延　吉	433
焦　作	391	四　平	434
三门峡	3891	**黑龙江省**	
湖北省		哈尔滨	451
武　汉	27	齐齐哈尔	452
黄　石	714	牡丹江	453
沙　市	716	佳木斯	454
宜　昌	717	大　庆	459
十　堰	719	**湖南省**	
襄　樊	710	长　沙	731
贵州省		湘　潭	732
贵　阳	851	株　州	733
遵　义	852	衡　阳	734
辽宁省		常　德	736
沈　阳	24	岳　阳	730
大　连	411	**广东省**	
鞍　山	412	广　州	20
抚　顺	413	汕　头	754
本　溪	414	深　圳	755
丹　东	415	珠　海	756

通达地点	长途区号	通达地点	长途区号
佛　山	757	南　京	25
湛　江	759	镇　江	511
东　莞	769	苏　州	512
顺　德	765	南　通	513
中　山	760	扬　州	514
广西壮族自治区		徐　州	516
南　宁	771	淮　阴	517
柳　州	772	常　州	519
桂　林	773	无　锡	510
梧　州	774	**浙江省**	
北　海	779	杭　州	571
阳　朔	773	嘉　兴	573
海南省		宁　波	574
海　口	898	绍　兴	575
四川省		温　州	577
成　都	28	**安徽省**	
重　庆	811	合　肥	551
自　贡	813	蚌　埠	552
绵　阳	816	芜　湖	553
南　充	817	马鞍山	555
宜　宾	831	安　庆	556
乐　山	833	黄　山	559
西　昌	834	**云南省**	
峨眉山	8426	昆　明	871
江苏省		个　旧	873

通达地点	长途区号
曲　靖	874
保　山	875
东　川	8811
西藏自治区	
拉　萨	891
陕西省	
西　安	29
延　安	911
汉　中	916
宝　鸡	917
咸　阳	910
甘肃省	
兰　州	931
武　威	935
张　掖	936
酒　泉	937

通达地点	长途区号
宁夏回族自治区	
天　水	938
敦　煌	9473
嘉峪关	9477
银　川	951
石嘴山	952
吴　忠	953
青海省	
西　宁	971
格尔木	979
新疆维吾尔自治区	
乌鲁木齐	991
石河子	993
吐鲁番	995
喀　什	998
克拉玛依	990

　　磁卡电话:预先购买磁卡,插入装有专门读卡器的磁卡电话上进行通话,磁卡电话机能按通话时间按收费标准自动计费,在磁卡电话机上可以打国际、国内长途电话和市内电话。电话磁卡在各大宾馆饭店及电信服务点均有出售,并相应设有磁卡电话。

国际邮电局

　　位于建国门北大街雅宝路。从建国门立交桥向北走大约 300 米。办理收寄国际、国内信函、包裹及特快邮件、开具兑付汇票、电报汇款、国际、国内电报、长途电话和市内电话。这里设有海关,可在交寄时办理海关手续。

电话:5128120 5128114

营业时间:8:00-19:00

交通:44 路,地铁。

邮电局

主要街区、火车站、机场、游览区都有邮电局。门窗和邮电局标志都是绿色的,全周营业。营业时间8:00-19:00。电报、电话、电传业务是 24 小时营业。

国内信件:寄往本市的信件贴 10 分邮票,外省为 20 分。手信重量不超过 20 克,里面只能装书信。信封左上方为收信人地址、邮政编码;右下方为寄信人地址、邮政编码。城市的要按省、市、区、街道、门牌号码及楼区住宅编号顺序写明;农村的要按省、市、县、乡、村等顺序写明。

国际航空手信根据地区和信重邮资不同,一般每封在 3.2 元以上,港台地区手信每封 2.6 元。各饭店、宾馆均有邮筒发国际、国内信件。

就医指南

北京有一批全国闻名的大型综合医院、专科医院,也有著名的中医医院。这些医院名医荟萃,医术高超。外地患者进京就医,主要是治疗疑难重症,或在当地医院治疗效果不太明显的疾病。来京求医,须携带有关的病历、诊断书、化验单、X 光片等,以便医生迅速了解患者病况，及时进行诊治，对症下药。北京有些医院，实行专家挂牌门诊，在告示上注明了专家名医的姓名、特长和诊治时间，以供病员作最佳选择。专家门诊挂号费，较之一般挂号费用要高出数倍，款额不等。每天早晨，到医院挂号的人数较多，须提前数小时到挂号处排队等候，以免耽误就诊。为使进京求医问药者心中有数，下面将北京若干医院情况加以概括介绍。

协和医院

久负盛名的综合性医院，全国解决疑难病症的技术指导中心。世界卫生组织国际疾病分类合作中心及中国医学科学院妇产科、内分泌科、核医学科、眼科四个研究中心设在该院。

地址：东城区帅府园 1 号，邮编：100730

电话：5295114

北京医院

综合性医院。以治疗各种老年性疾病为重点。

地址：东单大华路 1 号，邮编：100730

电话：5132266（总机）

中日友好医院

现代化的综合性医院。以中西医结合为特点，特色科室：普外科、胸外科、骨外科、消化内科、耳鼻喉科、皮肤科、中医内科、中医妇科、中医肿瘤科等。

地址：朝阳区樱花东路，邮编：100029

电话：4221122

同仁医院

市属综合性医院。以眼科、耳鼻喉科医疗为重点,该两科的一些医疗和手术居全国一流水平。

地址:崇文门内大街 2 号, 邮编:100730

电话:5129911

友谊医院

市级综合性医院。设热带医学研究所、临床医学研究所。特色科室为泌尿科,肾移植成功率居领先水平。

地址:宣武区永安路 95 号, 邮编:100050

电话:3014411

宣武医院

市级综合性医院。以老年病医疗、研究为特色,以心、脑疾病治疗见长。

地址:宣武区长椿街 45 号, 邮编 100053

电话:3013355

朝阳医院

市级综合性医院。呼吸疾病医疗研究中心设在该院。以呼吸系统疾病的医疗研究为重点,以临床生化检验质控、高压氧及职业病诊治为特色。

地址:朝外白家庄路 8 号, 邮编:100020

电话:5007755

积水潭医院

市级综合性医院。北京市创伤骨科研究所设在该院。以创伤骨科和烧伤科为重点,手外科、创伤骨科、骨肿瘤科、烧伤科医绩在国内外知名。

地址:新街口东街 31 号,邮编:100035

电话:6057631

天坛医院

市属大型综合性医院。以神经外科为重点,是亚洲规模最大的神经外科中心。

地址:天坛西里 6 号,邮编:100050

电话:7016611

北京中医医院

市级综合性中医医院,国内外享有盛名。以肝病科、内科、外科、儿科、皮科、肿瘤科、针灸科、按摩科见长。

地址:美术馆后街 23 号,邮编:100010

电话:4016677

北京儿童医院

市级综合性儿童医院。与联合国儿童基金会合作,负责中国地区儿童急救和儿童医师培训。

地址:南礼士路 56 号, 邮编:100045

电话:8528401

北京妇产医院

中国较大的妇产专科医院。对高危妊娠的及时识别和管理,对先天性畸形的宫内诊断、胎儿宫内发育监测,胎盘功能监测、分娩时机和方式的合理选择,对妊娠合并症等早期诊断和治疗,颇具特色。

地址:东城区骑河楼 17 号,邮编:100006

电话:5250731

北京口腔医院

市属口腔专科医院。

地址:天坛西里 4 号,邮编:100050

电话:7013355

阜外医院

主治心血管疾病的专科医院。以冠心病、高血压、先心病、瓣膜病、肺心病、大血管病等防治的临床医疗为主。

地址:北礼士路 167 号, 邮编:100073

电话:8314466

安定医院

市属精神卫生专科医院。老年精神病科、精神病学鉴定科、药物依赖性治疗康复科、儿童精神病科等国内有声誉。

地址:西城区德外安康胡同 5 号,邮编:100088

电话:2013330

肿瘤医院

中国医学科学院下属大型肿瘤专科医院。有些治疗达国际水平或国际领先水平。

地址:朝阳区潘家园,邮编:100021

电话:5113874

第一传染病医院

市级传染病专科医院。

地址:地坛公园 13 号, 邮编:100011

电话:4211031

北京急救中心

地址:前门西大街

电话:120

北京香港国际医务诊所

地址:朝阳门北大街 2 号

电话:5012288 - 2346

国际医疗中心

地址:燕莎中心 S106

电话:4651561

购 物

购物是旅行的一大乐趣,更是常驻北京之必需。旅行者在京购物首推富于东方特色和浓郁京味的工艺美术品及历代文物。长期作为帝都的北京,云集了各地能工巧匠,使北京的工艺品比较集中的体现了中华民族工艺之精华。被称为北京工艺美术品"四大名旦"的景泰兰、牙雕、玉器、雕漆以及金石篆刻、文房四宝、古玩字画、丝绸刺绣,珠宝翠瓒,巧夺天工,多姿多采。对偏爱民间手工艺品的人,北京的面人、泥人、绢人、脸谱、风筝、剪纸也是一绝。其他名特产品还有畅销全球的雪莲牌羊绒衫、天坛牌男衬衫、各种手编毛衣、金燕牌裘皮。北京的乐器也有极高制作水平,不少客人选购中国民间乐器,或学弹奏或作装饰。传统的中国家具近年也倍受青睐。典型的北京食品是各种蜜饯果脯和京味点心,北京的中药滋补品也更为正宗,货真价实。随着近年来的对外开放,大型购物中心的崛起,世界各地名牌商品以及日用百货也出现在北京的柜台。

王府井大街、前门、西单和东四是北京的四大商业区。王府井位于东长安街,已有百余年历史,不足一公里长的大街上商店密集,有著名的百货大楼以及全市最大的新华书店、工艺美术品商店、外文书店、妇女儿童用品商店,目前正与香港合资进行大规模的商业改造。

前门大街 500 年前就是北京的商业中心,老字号、小铺子多,更为北京市民所喜爱。

自天安门西行不远便是西单,被称为第二个王府井,有购物中心、食品商场、服装商场,商品齐全。

东四在王府井大街东北面,自旧时隆福寺庙会发展而来,有名的隆福小吃店就在此处。

银街位于东单北大街,许多世界名牌商品专卖店集中于此。

以上几处堪称京城锦绣之地,又有浓郁民俗风情,但美中不足的是名声大,人太多,购物十分拥挤。购物需上闹市,闹市也不只这几处,不少北京人买东西去新落成的购物中心或专卖店,不太挤、货色照样齐全,旅游者不妨一试。

北京商业区一般营业时间是 8:30 - 20:00,冬季 9:00 - 19:00,大的购物中心和友谊商店会延迟到晚 21:00,也不会象商业区那样拥挤。夜市大多在天将黑时开始。比较大的商场和被北京市旅游局定为旅游定点商店的购物场所,都有外汇兑换处或接受信用卡,在街头摊挡购物最好事先兑换好外币。

商店购物不用讲价,但如有时间,多走几家比较一下价格会更好,注意保存好你的收据,退换商品时用得上。在街头摊挡和一些个体小商店则尽可尝试一下您的讨价还价技巧。

若干大型商场

燕莎友谊商城

具有国际水平的大型商城,购物环境豪华舒适,经营国内外优质商品 30 万个品种。设有零售、批发及进出口贸易业务,和外币兑换、礼品镶、临时托幼、邮购函购、海内外托运等服务项目。

地址:朝阳区亮马桥路 52 号

电话:4651188(总机)

北京城乡贸易中心商场

是一座开业于 90 年代的现代化大型购物中心。商场内厅豪华、典雅。四层营业楼占地面积达 2 万平方米,荟萃全国各地名、特、优、新、精的高、中、低档三万多种商品。"宾客至上,服务第一,优质高效,争创一流"是这家商场的宗旨。

　　地址:复兴路甲 23 号

　　电话:8216582

西单商场

　　是具有 60 多年历史的商场,经过改扩建,营业面积达 3 万平方米,汇集种类新、优、名、特四万余种商品,是集购物、娱乐、餐饮为一体的大型综合性商业企业,以齐全的商品、优雅的环境、良好的服务享誉京城。

　　地址:西单北大街 120 号

　　电话:6056531(总机)

长安商场

　　是本市新建的现代化、多功能综合型大商场,营业面积 1.4 万平方米,经营百货食品等三万种名、特、优、新商品,并附设合资企业专柜及名店名厂产品柜,还根据顾客需要制定了百余项服务条款。

　　地址:复兴门外大街

　　电话:8528851(总机)

复兴商业城

　　集购物、餐饮、娱乐、服务于一体的大型现代化商城,附设富丽华酒楼、快餐厅和歌舞总会,总经营面积 1 万平方米。经营家电、服装、鞋帽、百货、食品等名、特、优、新商品三万余种,立百项服务措施。

　　地址:复兴门外大街 4 号楼

　　电话:8530142 8033740

贵友大厦

是以经营中、高档名牌商品为特色的购物场所,营业面积八千平方米。大厦以"商品迎人,服务暖人,环境宜人"为经营宗旨,竭诚为中外宾客提供优质服务,贵友连续被北京市评为"商品服务好、售后服务好"单位。

地址:北京建国门外大街甲5号

电话:5011177(总机)

北京百货大楼

国营大型商业企业,经营商品50大类、三万多种,以中高档为主,以品类齐全著称。日接待顾客达十几万人次。共四层营业厅,四楼附建"友谊服务部"设酒吧、舞厅、餐厅等。百货大楼连续获得北京市和全国的先进单位、红旗单位称号。

地址:王府井大街

电话:5126677(总机)

蓝岛大厦

本市新建的现代化、多功能综合性大型涉外商业中心,集购物、美食、文化娱乐于一体。商厦建筑典雅别致,设施先进豪华,购物环境优美舒适,经营国内外名、优、精、新商品近三万个品种,采用多样方式为顾客服务。

地址:朝阳门外大街8号(东大桥路口)

电话:5044422(总机)

天桥百货商场

本市著名大型综合商场之一,曾被国家授予全国第一面商业红旗称号,改革开放以来亦走在前列。1992年扩建成一座富丽堂皇的现代化商贸大厦,场内设施先进完备,购物环境舒适优美,经营商品种类齐全,优质服务众口皆碑,订有为顾客服务的多项措施。

地址:永定门内大街

电话:3043377(总机)

天元购物中心

原和平商业大厦,经营种类名优商品三万余种,设施现代化,售后服务优质,遵循"宁肯企业受损,不让顾客吃亏"的经营准则。

地址:和平里中街17号

电话:4213320

隆福大厦

隆福大厦股份有限公司是一座综合性现代化的商业大厦,大厦主楼地下一层及地上一至六楼营业,经营商品达3万多种。大厦设施齐全,功能完善,还设有地下超级市场、麦当劳隆福餐厅等。

地址:隆福寺街95号

电话:4012037

北京友谊商店

是以外宾、华侨和港澳台胞为主要服务对象的大型综合商场。经营国产和进口商品,种类齐全,特别是久负盛名的中国丝绸、金银首饰、珠宝钻翠、牙雕玉刻、刺绣、景泰蓝、文房四宝、古玩字画、海关手续等服务。

地址:建国门外大街
电话:5003311(总机)

名特产品

文物古董

许多人把在北京购买文物当作旅行目的之一。北京作为六朝故都,文物资源极为丰富。位于和平门的琉璃厂文化街已有 500 年历史,是选购文物的好地方。由政府正式批准出售文物的商店大都坐落此处,晚清建筑风格的店铺鳞次栉比,著名的荣宝斋出售历代名人字画、文房四宝。中国书店为中国最大的古旧书籍商店,钱币商店专营历代古币,文物商店及其各个分号出售古代竹、木、牙雕、瓷器、玉器、中式家具等。此外,位于东单的华夏工艺品商店和友谊商店也出售各类文物。最近,北京市文物局又批准了 6 个经营民间古旧货品的交易市场,吸引了大批海外人士。在这里徜徉于丰富多彩的民间古旧货品之间,讨价还价,沙里淘金,别有一番乐趣。除以上推荐商店外,各三星级以上酒店商场都有工艺品专柜,出售精美货品。

鉴别文物真假的最好办法是看所购买的物品上是否有"京文检"标记。我们向您所推荐的场所购买文物都具有这种检验标记,在为您出具的正式收据上会标明物品名称及年代。1795－1949 年间的文物携带出境之前需要携带所购物品及其收据到设在友谊商店的文物局办公室加盖火漆,办公时间为每周一下午2:00 – 5:00。

丝绸

在北京可以买到各种丝绸布料、内、外衣、床上用品、装饰品等。

优质的丝绸还可以在友谊商店,大的购物中心以及酒店商场中买到。位于永安里的秀水街市场和雅宝路市场出售各种丝绸衣裙、内衣、睡衣、羽绒服及床上用品。经营者均为个体摊商,交易方式灵活,很多摊商会讲英语,大部分为出口转内销商品,尺寸大多为西方尺码,已经成为海外游客的必到之处。

地毯

除了传统京味地毯外,北京还可以购买到内蒙、新疆、江浙等地毯产地的优质产品。

食品/烟酒/日用百货

北京各类进口、国产食品、饮料、化妆品及家庭日用品货源丰富,大型购物中心及综合服务设施中均有超级市场供应上述物品。

药品

中药店除出售药品之外还出售传统的中药补品,百货公司或超级市场也有药品专柜。

书籍

作为中国文化中心,北京每年出版2万多种书籍及1300多种期刊,北京外文书店及其7个分店出售各种外文书刊,北京新华书店共有 200 多个分店,除可以买到各类图书外,还有录音带、录像带、激光唱盘以及小工艺品、贺年卡等。许多海外人士特别是来自香港、澳门、台湾的客人,喜欢在京购书,不仅种类多而且价格便宜。

购物指南

文物古董

北京友谊商店	华夏工艺品分店
地址:建国门外 17 号	地址:王府井 293 号
电话:5003311	电话:5251819

华夏工艺品商店
地址:东单
电话:5247303

民间古旧货品交易市场一般营业时间为 9:00 - 19:00

琉璃厂海王村旧货市场	劲松工艺品旧货市场
琉璃厂古文化街	朝外旧货市场
琉璃厂荣宝斋后荣兴艺廊	什刹海旧货市场
天坛公园北门红桥市场	皇城根旧货市场

工艺品珠宝首饰

友谊商店	华夏艺术品分店
地址:建国门外大街 17 号	地址:王府井大街 293 号
电话:5003311	电话:5251819

白孔雀艺术世界
地址:德外北滨河

电话:2011199

华夏艺术品商店
地址:东单
电话:5136204

北京玉器厂外宾服务部
地址:崇文区光明路 11 号
电话:7027371 转 371

华萃礼品宫
地址:新外新康大街 5 号
电话:2025857

中国工艺美术品展销公司
地址:西直门北京展览馆
西二馆
电话:8316677 转 4323

中国工艺美术馆
地址:复兴门立交桥
电话:6013377

亮马商场
地址:北三环东路
电话:5016688 转 5678

书画

荣宝斋
地址:西琉璃厂 19 号

燕京书画社
地址:天坛公园内祈年殿
门市部
电话:7025262

炎黄艺术馆
地址:亚运村 9 号
电话:4911046

王府书画店
地址:王府井大街 67 号
电话:5133629

丝绸

元隆丝绸股份有限公司
地址：天坛路 55 号

北京国际丝绸商店
地址：朝阳区安外安慧里
402 号

电话：7012854

电话：4914185

北京丝绸商店
地址：前门大街珠宝市 5 号
电话：3016658

友谊商店
地址：建外大街 17 号
电话：5003311

地毯

北京地毯贸易中心
地址：梁家庄苇子坑 90 号
电话：7616018

燕莎友谊商城
地址：朝阳区亮马桥路 52 号
电话：4651188

懋隆地毯商店
地址：国贸商场二层
电话：5051974

华夏工艺品商店
地址：王府井大街 293 号
电话：5251819

中式仿古及古旧家俱

北京中式家俱厂
地址：永定门外大街 64 号
电话：7223344

友谊商店
地址：建外大街 17 号
电话：5003311

白孔雀艺术世界
地址：德外北滨河路
电话：2011199

家居及办公家具

北京中式家具厂
地址:永定门外大街 64 号
电话:7223344

赛特购物中心家具部
地址:建外大街 22 号
电话:5124488

复兴商业城
地址:西长安街
电话:8534512

军事博物馆
地址:海淀区复兴路 9 号
电话:8514357

方庄开隆家具城
地址:丰台区方庄蒲方
路东口

天坛家具城
地址:五棵松路 32 号

卫艺红木家具城

地址:东交民巷 37 号

食品/日用品

国贸惠康超级市场
赛特超级市场
丽都超级市场
燕莎超级市场
百盛超级市场
协和百货平价市场

药店

同仁堂药店
地址:宣武区大栅栏 24 号
电话:3032871

王府井医药商店
地址:王府井大街 267 号
电话:5252322

前门药店
地址:前门大街 34 号
电话:5113303

长春堂药店
前门大街

乐仁堂药店
西单北大街

东单药店
东单北大街 97 号

怀仁堂药店
西四北大街

保和堂药店
北京站前街 16 号

宏仁堂药店
东四北大街 434 号

千芝堂中药店
崇文门外大街

和平里药店
和平里西街

万全堂药店
崇外大街 35 号

华安医药商店
崇文门内大街 21 号

北京新药特药商店
东四北大街

永安堂药店

朝阳门内大街 366 号

东城区药材公司东城药品
批发商店
东四九条 73 号

东城区百草参茸药材公司
王府井大街 136 号

白塔寺药店
阜内大街 165 号

鹤年堂中药店

德寿堂药店

宣武区菜市口　　　　　珠市口西大街 175 号

鹤鸣堂药店　　　　　　圣济堂药店
骡马市大街 83 号　　　西直门内大街 145 号

南庆仁堂药店　　　　　天桥中药店
前门南大街 128 号　　　天桥市场西街 47 号

书店
王府井外文书店
琉璃厂文化街
西单外文书店
西单购物中心精品书店

眼镜
大明眼镜店　　　　　　同仁验光配镜中心
地址:王府井大街 297 号　地址:崇文门南大街 2 号

精益眼镜店　　　　　　百盛购物中心小林眼镜店
地址:宣武门南大街 114 号　地址:百盛购物中心

图章
翠文阁艺术篆刻门市部　首都刻字厂
地址:琉璃厂东街　　　地址:珠市口西大街 258 号

印痕楼治印社
地址:南新华街 45 号

邮票

中国集邮总公司　　　　　月坛集邮品市场
地址:宣武门东大街 2 号　地址:月坛公园内

美容院

四联美容美发中心　　　　丽人美容院
电话:5255281　　　　　　电话:5150358/5052288 转
　　　　　　　　　　　　2182

皇后美容中心　　　　　　温莎美容院
电话:5257059　　　　　　电话:5126321

Roger Craig　　　　　　　新红装美容健康俱乐部
电话:5052266/5128899　电话:4617038

旗袍

明星中式服装店　　　　　名人旗袍加工部
地址:王府井大街 133 号　地址:东单北大街 12 号
电话:5257945　　　　　　电话:5224936

北京丝绸商店
地址:前门大街珠宝市 5 号
电话:3016658

美 食

　　北京是集全国美味之大全的首善之区,街上餐馆
上千家,其中名店上百个,并各有几个拿手好菜。如

果您想念异国家乡菜,北京还有正宗的法式、美式、意大利式、俄式西餐厅和日本料理、韩国烧烤以及越南、印尼、泰国风味。

在街上餐馆用膳,通常会比较便宜,营业时间一般是上午10:00至下午2:00,下午4:00至晚8:00。一般来说餐馆人比较多。但对外宾和港澳台同胞来说,倘若只有几个人,餐馆一般都会优先照顾。菜单大都有中英文对照。

各餐馆都有装修讲究、优雅的单间,并接受电话订座,但也常是供不应求。尤其是在旅游旺季,需要提前预订。

酒店内和酒店外的风味餐馆一般都收信用卡和支票。

中 餐

北京菜

"京菜"擅长烤、爆、烧、闷、涮。"北京烤鸭"是游客来京必食的美味。"全聚德"的挂炉烤鸭用明火烤;"便宜坊"的闷炉烤鸭用暗火烤,两种"流派"各有千秋。通红发亮的烤鸭片成片,蘸甜面酱加葱卷在特制的荷叶饼里,吃起来香甜可口。

"烤肉季"、"烤肉宛"的烤肉是把浸透佐料的牛羊肉片放在铁灸上烤,边烤边吃,别具情趣。

涮羊肉是最受北京人欢迎的冬令美食。以"东来顺"、"又一顺"、"能人居"的涮羊肉名气最大。尤其是冬天,一家人围着沸腾的火锅,把羊肉片在锅里涮一涮,蘸上特别的佐料,真是红红火火,大饱口福。

宫庭菜

　　源于宫廷帝妃的御用菜。皇家食谱自然气派不凡,异常讲究。

　　菜馔以清、鲜、香、嫩为特色。"仿膳"和"听鹂馆"是最正宗的两家,一家在北海公园内,一家在颐和园,都是过去皇帝的御膳房。当年的老师傅传下技艺。在这儿,皇帝吃过什么,您也可以吃到什么,连屋里的摆设都是宫庭式样,别有一番豪华气派。

四川菜

　　中国最大的菜系,全中国至少有十分之一人爱吃四川菜。川菜辛辣诱人,兼有麻、甜、咸、酸、苦、香、怪数种味道,享有一菜一格、百菜百味的美誉。北京资格最老的川菜馆,当数坐落在宣武门内绒线胡同一所古老的深宅大院中的"四川饭店"。而"豆花饭庄"规模虽小却有特色,飞檐小楼中木桌木椅,那穿着印花裤褂的四川妹子,手提铜壶、一身四川打扮的"茶博士"都会让您觉着置身于天府之国。

潮州菜

　　潮州位于沿海区城,自然以海鲜著名。举凡名贵的龙虾、海螺、花蟹、大鳝……都有独特的烹调方法,使之成为桌上珍馐。富乡土风味的家常小菜搬上酒楼,不致失礼,反觉纯朴可喜,也是潮菜的特色之一。

　　名贵的鱼翅和燕窝往往是潮州菜馆的招牌菜,专用蘸汁也是潮州菜的特色,如卤水鹅配菜蒜茸醋、清蒸龙虾配桔汁、鱼饭(冷吃的蒸鱼)配普宁豆酱,使佳看更添美味,以小壶小杯装盛功夫茶奉客,是潮州菜馆的必备项目,目的不在表演,而在帮助食客的消化。

粤菜

有人说粤菜是世界上味道最鲜美的菜,不算过份。它是特点是清淡、生脆、爽口,擅长海鲜。客人可以在鱼缸内选择活蹦乱跳的鲜鱼当场烹制。东江豆腐、梅菜扣肉是他的代表作,粤式点心款式繁多,深受人们喜爱。老字号大三元,新崛起的阿静粤菜馆,都有地道的粤菜,而豪华的渔都海鲜城、顺峰海鲜酒楼由香港名厨师主理,更使北京人享受到地道的海鲜大菜。

江苏菜

1921年开业的"玉华台"名气最大。它的鳝鱼席和名色小吃点心、蟹壳黄、淮扬汤包等具有清淡适口、甜咸适中的特色。

江苏风味还包括著名的杭州菜,以鲜嫩味美的叫化童鸡、西湖醋鱼为代表,是典型的江南风味。

上海菜

比起粤菜,上海菜的口味较为浓郁、油腻及略甜。

上海的泡菜和咸肉极为著名,其中皮蛋更是驰名的小吃。大闸蟹是上海最有名的食品,其他如八宝鸭、醉鸡、炒鳝糊和糟溜黄鱼等,都是沪菜精品。

山西菜

最有名的菜是过油肉、香酥肥鸭,并以面食花样多著称,面食小点心令人叫绝。北京最大的山西风味餐厅是晋阳饭庄,位于珠市口西大街 241 号。

山东菜

北京人的家常菜受山东风味影响最大,街上山东馆子也最多。著名的"丰泽园"在前门外,"孔膳堂"在琉璃厂文化街,当年的鲁国人孔夫子讲究"食不厌精、脍不厌细",他到底吃什么,您去尝尝就知道了。

湖南菜

湘菜的口味和川菜近同,以辣椒、大蒜为主要配料。湘菜还有一种"怪味酱",使菜的味道更为浓郁。

湖南的汤羹异常香浓,包括面条汤、清炖鸽子及曲园豌豆羹;而竹节盅及湖南赤陶汤匙更是别致的餐具。至于湖南特产莲花和百合,往往组合成绝妙的甜品。

朝鲜菜

狗肉条、狗肉汤、烤鱼、各种各样的泡菜。朝鲜冷面的凉、辣、甜、香是很多人喜爱的风味。朝鲜烧烤是北京人冬天最喜爱的风味之一。亮马大厦、燕莎中心的萨拉伯尔、赛特俱乐部的亚里廊都是正宗的朝鲜风味餐厅,并有朝鲜族小姐服务。

新疆菜

"吐鲁番餐厅"的烤全羊是最有代表性的,烤好的整只羊,昂首挺胸、通体金黄,特邀维族名厨烹制,趁热挥刀切片,顿时满屋生香。

蒙古菜

以烧、烤为主,原料主要是牛、羊肉。在"锡林郭勒餐厅"和"成吉思汗酒家"可以吃到正宗的烤羊腿、手抓肉。

药膳

用珍贵的人参、鹿茸、熊掌、枸杞、甲鱼等制成菜肴。"西苑养生斋"深得食客赞誉。

清真

北京有许多回族人,清真餐馆生意兴隆。老字号"鸿云楼"、"鸿宾楼",都有美味的牛羊肉菜肴和全素席。

火锅

由于北京冬季寒冷,火锅始终是北京人的桌上宠物。近年来粤式火锅、四川火锅大举北上,与传统的京式涮羊肉(蒙古火锅)一同走俏京城,使旅京人士大饱口福。各式火锅所涮原料多为牛、羊肉片、各式海鲜和新鲜蔬菜,相对来讲,粤式火锅锅底、调料较为清淡,川式火锅则以麻辣见长。不少餐馆和酒店推出自助火锅,很受欢迎。

怀旧风味

怀旧风味是近年来在饮食习惯变化和怀旧心理作用下餐饮业新出现的一批富于特色的餐厅,它包括折射文革时代的"向阳屯"、"黑土地"、"黄土地"等,也包括返璞归真令人耳目一新的"燧人氏"、"半坡火锅啤酒村",如有朋友相伴,在这里用餐则更能贴近北京人的情感与当今时尚。

京味小吃

北京风味小吃有 600 多年历史,由于兼收各民族小吃特色,品种十分丰富。街上有许多小吃店,夜市和自由市场也有专售风味小吃的摊档。到了春节,庙会、花会上的小吃摊可算是最吸引人的地方。目前,在北京能吃到的小吃有:焦圈、豌豆黄、麻花、豆面糕、炸糕、年糕、豆腐脑、茶汤、油炒面、艾窝窝、烤白薯、豆汁、炒肝、馄饨、炒疙瘩等。另外还有节令小吃,如元宵在元宵节(每年一月)前后上市,粽子则是在端午节前后能吃到。

欧陆菜式

法餐

法式烹饪自上世纪之初即闻名全球。经典法式烹饪中含多种令人百吃不厌的菜式,包括法式洋葱汤、水煮牛肉、红酒烩肉,以及法国各地风行的多种土豆类菜式和甜品。

现代法餐奉行真料简烹的准则。各种原料只是"略做加工",佐以轻淡调汁和时蔬,尽量发挥食料原来品味,而且最大限度地保存其营养成分。

除此之外,莫忘一名法国成语:"没有葡萄酒的日子是没有阳光的日子"。想做个有品味的葡萄酒鉴赏家吗? 请记住:"只相信您自己的舌头"。

建国饭店的 Justine's 是京城最好的欧陆餐饮场

所,由法厨亲自拟订食单。

意大利餐

世界上最流行的烹饪术之一。意式菜汤、烩小牛骨、火腿小牛肉和冰淇淋及甜品风行五大洲。自然,还不应忘记比萨饼。

米饭和意式面食每餐都不可少。肉类菜很丰富,如小牛肉配银鱼汁、炸火腿卷等。意大利毗邻地中海,海鲜烹饪有其独特功夫。

意大利红葡萄酒也全球闻名。其它各种佐餐酒也口味独特,包括多种苦艾酒,如马蒂尼酒。

京城优秀的意式餐厅有中等价位的贡多拉(凯宾斯基饭店)和 Pinocchio Pizzeria(丽都假日饭店)及高价位罗马餐厅(王府饭店)。

美国餐

美国烹饪起源于早期移民的多种饮食习俗。比如,风行于新奥尔良和路易斯安那地区的烹饪术,实际上受到法国、西班牙、非洲和当地土著人烹调方法的多重影响。

人们普遍认为当今美国烹调的"麦加"是加利福尼亚州。同新时代法厨一样,加州厨师只选用上佳原料,辅以多种烹调手法,创立了所谓"环太平洋烹饪"的新流派。

京城目前最地道的美式餐厅当数希尔顿酒店的"路易斯安那",可以说它和 Jusitine's 是北京欧陆餐厅中的双碧。

瑞士餐

　　瑞士烹饪实际上是周边邻国食式的混合体,当然也有自身独特的菜式,特别是各式冷肠,奶酪和巧克力。

　　甜品种类繁多,每个地区都有自己独有的风味,如图高地区的苹果馅饼,左格地区的樱桃果仁蛋糕,及恩加丁的胡核馅饼。

　　港澳中心瑞士酒店和国都大饭店均有地道的瑞士餐厅,同时提供种类多样的红、白葡萄酒。

德国餐

　　德国以其拥有世界上种类最繁多的香肠而闻名。一般来说食量供应充足,又有啤酒或白葡萄酒佐餐。

　　北京最受欢迎的德国餐厅是凯宾斯基饭店的德国啤酒屋,屋中有自设的啤酒坊,供应新鲜啤酒。

北京烤鸭

和平门烤鸭店

前门大街 14 号

营业时间:10:30 - 13:30

　　　　　　16:30 - 20:00

电话:3018833

前门烤鸭店

前门大街 32 号

营业时间:11:30 - 13:30

　　　　　　17:30 - 19:30

电话:7016321

便宜坊烤鸭店

崇文门外大街 2 号

营业时间:19:00 - 21:00

电话:7012244 转 342

北京烤鸭店

团结湖北口 3 楼

营业时间:11:00 - 21:00

　　　　　　16:30 - 19:30

电话:5072892

前门外鲜鱼口内 113 号
营业时间:11:00 - 14:00
　　　　　16:30 - 20:00
电话:5112092

利康烤鸭店
朝外工体南路 1 号
营业时间:10:30 - 13:30
　　　　　16:30 - 19:30
电话:5023745

京信烤鸭店
东三环北路甲 2 号
营业时间:10:30 - 13:30
　　　　　17:30 - 20:00
电话:4660895

王府井烤鸭店
帅府园 13 号
营业时间:10:30 - 13:30
　　　　　16:30 - 19:30
电话:5253310

宫庭菜
仿膳饭庄
北海公园
营业时间:11:00 - 14:00
　　　　　17:00 - 19:30
电话:4011879

御膳饭庄
天坛路 87 号
营业时间:11:00 - 14:00
　　　　　16:00 - 19:30
电话:7014263

活鱼酒家
工体东路甲 6 号

汇珍楼饭庄
北辰东路 8 号

营业时间:10:30-19:30

电话:5003794

听鹂馆饭庄

颐和园

营业时间:11:00-14:00
　　　　　17:00-19:00

电话:2581955

古都精典

北京贵宾楼饭店

营业时间:11:30-14:00
　　　　　18:00-22:00

电话:5137788 转 347

历家菜

德内大街羊房胡同 11 号

预订:提前 2 周

电话:6011915

凯莱宫

凯莱大酒店

营业时间:18:30-20:45

电话:5158855 转 3331

营业时间:11:00-14:00
　　　　　17:00-22:00

电话:4993285

宫廷大酒店

昌平西关

营业时间:18:00-21:00

电话:9744728

沙锅居

西四南大街 60 号

营业时间:10:30-13:30
　　　　　17:00-20:00

电话:6021126

云来堂谭家菜

北京饭店

营业时间:11:30-14:00
　　　　　18:00-20:30

电话:5137766 转 1389

广东菜

御香苑
粤海皇都酒店
营业时间:11:30－14:30
　　　　　17:30－22:00
电话:5136666 转 2216

明珠海鲜酒家
地安门大街 111 号
营业时间:11:00－14:00
　　　　　17:00－22:30
电话:4035888

大阪徐园餐厅
南河沿 86 号
营业时间:11:00－14:00
　　　　　17:00－21:00
电话:5130972

世界美食中心
南河沿华龙街 82 号
营业时间:11:00－14:00
　　　　　17:00－22:00
电话:5126979

香港美食城
东安门大街 18 号
营业时间:11:00－14:30
　　　　　17:00－22:30
电话:5136668

港潮醉粤楼
北京饭店
营业时间:11:30－14:00
　　　　　17:30－21:00
电话:5137766 转 379

阿静粤菜馆
东四北大街轿子胡同 48
电话:4016712,4034181

大三元酒家
景山西街 50 号
营业时间:7:30－14:00
　　　　　17:00－20:00
电话:4013920

人人大酒楼
前门东大街 18 号

香满楼酒家
琉璃厂 4 号

营业时间:11:30 - 14:00
　　　　　17:30 - 21:30
电话:5112978

世界之窗餐厅
国际大厦
营业时间:11:45 - 15:00
　　　　　17:30 - 22:00
电话:5002255 转 2828

香港美食城分店
海淀区黄庄 31C
营业时间:10:00 - 14:30
　　　　　16:30 - 22:00
电话:2567015

华苑餐厅
华润饭店
营业时间:12:00 - 14:30
　　　　　17:30 - 21:30
电话:5012233 转 288

翠竹园
国都茂盛宾饭店

营业时间:11:30 - 14:00
　　　　　17:30 - 21:30
电话:3014156

美丽华翠亨村茶寮
建外大街 24 号
营业时间:11:00 - 15:00
　　　　　17:00 - 22:00
电话:5158833

锦园餐厅
昆仑饭店
营业时间:11:30 - 14:00
　　　　　17:30 - 21:30
电话:5003388 转 5693

牡丹苑
长富宫饭店
营业时间:7:00 - 9:00
　　　　　11:30 - 13:45
　　　　　17:30 - 21:45

电话:5125555 转 1035

龙宫
凯宾斯基饭店

营业时间:11:45－14:30
　　　　　18:00－22:30
电话:4565588 转 1415

潮阳舫(湖)
北京展览馆宾馆
营业时间:11:00－14:30
　　　　　17:30－22:00
电话:8316633 转 7024

夏宫
中国大饭店
营业时间:11:30－14:15
　　　　　18:00－21:45
电话:5052266 转 34

四季厅
建国饭店
营业时间:11:30－14:00
　　　　　18:00－22:00
电话:5002233 转 8041

潮都城
新大都饭店
营业时间:11:00－14:00
　　　　　17:00－22:30
电话:8319988 转 15126

营业时间:11:20－14:00
　　　　　17:30－22:00
电话:4653388 转 5712

满福楼
京广中心
营业时间:11:30－14:30
　　　　　17:30－22:00
电话:5018888 转 2599

越秀厅
王府饭店
营业时间:11:30－14:30
　　　　　18:00－21:00
电话:5128899 转 7405

福升阁海鲜酒家
赛特饭店
营业时间:11:30－14:30
　　　　　17:30－22:00
电话:5123388 转 2224

快活谷
港澳中心瑞士酒店
营业时间:11:30－14:00
　　　　　17:30－22:30
电话:5012288 转 2146

商人俱乐部餐厅
北京亚洲大酒店
营业时间:6:30 - 9:00
　　　　　11:30 - 14:30
　　　　　17:30 - 21:30
电话:5007788 转 7205

清风阁
兆龙饭店
营业时间:11:30 - 14:30
　　　　　17:30 - 22:00
电话:5002299

东篱
皇冠假日饭店
营业时间:11:30 - 14:00
　　　　　17:30 - 22:00
电话:5133388 转 1127

桃李餐厅
京伦饭店
营业时间:11:30 - 14:30
　　　　　17:30 - 22:00
电话:5002266

船
凯莱大酒店

明园
北京贵宾楼饭店
营业时间:11:00 - 14:00
　　　　　18:00 - 22:00
电话:5137788 转 344

酒仙阁
丽都假日饭店
营业时间:11:30 - 14:00
　　　　　18:00 - 22:00
电话:4376688 转 1700

珠江楼
新世纪饭店
营业时间:11:30 - 14:30
　　　　　17:30 - 22:00
电话:8491155

梅厅
梅地亚中心
营业时间:11:30 - 14:00
　　　　　18:00 - 21:30
电话:8514422 转 4173

四季厅
天伦王朝饭店

营业时间:11:30 - 14:30
　　　　　17:30 - 21:45
电话:5158855 转 3355

营业时间:11:30 - 13:45
　　　　　17:30 - 21:45
电话:5138888 转 8136

香宫
北京香格里拉饭店
营业时间:11:30 - 14:00
　　　　　17:30 - 22:00
电话:8412211 转 2732

随园
北京希尔顿酒店
营业时间:11:30 - 14:00
　　　　　17:30 - 22:00
电话:4662288 转 7416

恬园
金朗大酒店
营业时间:7:30 - 20:45
电话:5132288 转 5535

华兴宫
新大都饭店
电话:8319988 转 15118

海阳宫酒楼
民族饭店

营业时间:11:30 - 14:30
　　　　　17:30 - 22:30
电话:6014466 转 632

隆福酒楼
鼓楼东大街 167 号隆福大
厦宾馆内
营业时间:11:00 - 13:30
　　　　　17:00 - 20:30
电话:4059944 转 3407

顺峰餐厅
东三环路 16 号
电话:5071447

渔都海鲜城
工人体育场东门
电话:5085845

食街
京广新世界饭店
电话:5018888 转 2534

潮州菜

佳宁娜潮州酒楼
东华门大街 16 号
营业时间:11:30 - 14:30
　　　　　17:30 - 22:30
电话:5124373

潮江春
王府饭店
营业时间:11:30 - 14:30
　　　　　17:30 - 22:00
电话:5128899 转 7576

潮州海鲜酒家
首都大酒店
营业时间:11:30 - 14:00
　　　　　17:30 - 22:00
电话:5129988 转 3583

潮明园
和平宾馆
营业时间:11:30 - 14:30
　　　　　17:30 - 3:30
电话:5128833 转 6702

瑞麟楼海鲜酒家
复兴路甲 23 号城乡贸易
中心 5 段 3 楼
营业时间:11:00 - 14:30
　　　　　17:30 - 22:00
电话:8216542,8216567

鸿运燕翅楼
长城饭店
营业时间:11:30 - 14:30
　　　　　18:00 - 22:00
电话:5005566 转 2237

四川菜

来今雨轩
中山公园内

四川饭店
西绒线胡同 51 号

对外不营业,只对
旅行社、散客预订
电话:6056676

营业时间:11:00－14:00
　　　　　16:30－20:00
电话:6033291

峨嵋酒家
月坛北街 4 号
营业时间:10:30－14:00
　　　　　16:30－19:30
电话:8523069

豆花饭庄
广渠门外马圈
营业时间:11:00－13:30
　　　　　17:00－20:00
电话:7718392, 7712672

重庆园林酒家
天坛公园
团队包餐,散客预订
营业时间:11:30－14:30
　　　　　17:00－19:00
电话:7025825

渝园饭庄
日坛公园内(最好预订)
营业时间:11:00－14:00
　　　　　17:00－20:00
电话:5025985

花竹餐厅
前门东大街 2 号
电话:5122702

金沙阁中餐厅
新世纪饭店
营业时间:11:30－14:30
　　　　　17:30－22:00
电话:8491159

嘉陵楼
王府饭店

蓉园
贵宾楼饭店

营业时间:12:00－14:30
　　　　　18:00－21:30
电话:5128899 转 7900

颐园
北京饭店
营业时间:11:00－7:00
电话:5137766 转 1363

市井食街
兆龙饭店
营业时间:11:00－14:00
　　　　　17:30－22:00
电话:5002299

四环酒楼(新派)
海淀区太平路 27 号
四环宾馆内
营业时间:11:00－14:00
　　　　　17:00－21:00
电话:8235599

金太阳美食大酒楼(新派)
海淀区五棵松路口
往北 500 米

营业时间:11:30－14:00
　　　　　17:30－21:30
电话:5137788 转 340

四川餐厅
国贸中心
营业时间:11:30－14:00
　　　　　17:30－21:00
电话:5052288 转 6223

云台餐厅
长城饭店
营业时间:11:30－14:00
　　　　　18:00－22:00
电话:5005566 转 2162

楼上楼酒家
海淀区复兴路甲 23 号城
乡贸易中心大厦 5/F
营业时间:11:00－13:30
　　　　　17:00－20:00
电话:8216573,8216572

京人大酒店
(传统川菜)

营业时间:11:00 - 14:00　　营业时间:11:00 - 14:00
　　　　　17:00 - 21:00　　　　　　　17:00 - 21:00
电话:8217754　　　　　　　电话:8218586,8285381

帅府饭庄
什刹海前海北沿甲 19 号(北海后门)
营业时间:11:00 - 14:00
　　　　　17:30 - 21:00
电话:6058632,6058643

山东菜

聚山楼饭庄　　　　　　　香蜜湖酒家
鼓楼大街黄寺　　　　　　虎坊桥 3 号门前
营业时间:10:30 - 13:30　营业时间:11:00 - 14:00
　　　　　16:30 - 19:30

墨西哥

阿尔弗雷德
粤海皇都酒店
营业时间:17:30 - 02:00
电话:5136666 转 2133

北欧

北欧扒房　　　　　　　　皇室咖啡座
北京皇家大饭店　　　　　北京皇家大饭店
营业时间:18:30 - 22:00　营业时间:6:00 - 01:00
电话:4663388 转 3420　　电话:4663388

瑞士

瑞士餐厅

国都茂盛宾饭店

营业时间:18:00 - 22:30

电话:4565588 转 2

瑞士咖啡厅

港澳中心

营业时间:24 小时

电话:5012288 转 2127

快餐

加州牛肉面大王

东四西大街 26 号

亚痰时间:09:30 - 14:00

　　　　　17:00 - 21:00

电话:4669733

丽都快餐城

前门西大街正阳市场 1 号

营业时间:11:00 - 14:00

　　　　　17:00 - 21:00

电话:4919313

牡丹厅

梅地亚中心

营业时间:11:30 - 14:00

　　　　　18:00 - 21:00

电话:8514422 转 4255

孔膳堂饭庄

琉璃厂西街 3 号

营业时间:10:30 - 14:00

　　　　　16:30 - 20:00

电话:3030689

鲁味斋

北京展览馆宾馆

营业时间:11:30 - 14:30

　　　　　17:30 - 22:00

电话:8316633 转 7010

渔家宴大酒楼

和平门琉璃厂

电话:3047541

东北菜

吉隆餐厅

好运大世界餐厅

朝阳区安苑北里 25 号
楼吉林大厦内
营业时间:16:30 - 9:00
　　　　　11:30 - 14:00
　　　　　17:30 - 22:30
电话:4912704

龙港餐厅
复兴门北大街甲 5 号
黑龙江宾馆
营业时间:11:00 - 14:00
　　　　　17:00 - 21:00
特色:筋饼系列
电话:8525511 转 1013

饺子
品香饺子屋
五棵松北路玉松旅馆处
营业时间:10:00 - 24:00
特色:饺子宴
电话:8233831

清真菜
烤肉季饭庄
前海东沿 14 号
营业时间:10:30 - 13:30
　　　　　16:30 - 20:00
电话:4012170

西城区西四北大街 152 号

营业时间:11:00 - 24:00

特色:大马哈鱼
电话:6058924,6071643

鱼宴
朝阳区安华里三区十一
号楼
营业时间:全天
电话:4238431,4254085

吐鲁番餐厅
珠市口西大街 191 号
营业时间:11:30 - 14:00
　　　　　17:00 - 20:30
电话:3033167

鸿宾楼饭庄
西长安街 82 号
营业时间:10:30 – 14:00
　　　　　16:30 – 20:00
电话:6038460

西来顺饭庄
阜成门内大街 194 号
电话:6015996

又一顺饭庄
宣武门内大街 9 号
营业时间:10:30 – 20:30
电话:6022668

清真斋
西苑饭店
营业时间:12:00 – 14:00
　　　　　18:00 – 21:00
电话:8313388 转 5150

宣武门内大街 102 号
营业时间:10:30 – 13:00
　　　　　16:30 – 20:00
电话:6057707

北京同盛祥牛羊肉泡漠馆
王府井南口
营业时间:11:00 – 14:30
　　　　　17:00 – 21:00
电话:5243691

淮阳菜

淮扬春饭店
三里河东路 10 号
营业时间:9:30 – 13:30
　　　　　16:30 – 19:30
电话:8511224

如意饭庄(苏)
颐和园宾馆
营业时间:10:00 – 14:30
电话:2581803

老正兴饭庄
前门大街 46 号

淮扬餐厅
国贸中心

营业时间:10:30 - 13:30
　　　　　16:30 - 20:00
电话:5112145

中华礼仪餐厅
北京饭店
营业时间:7:00 - 9:00
　　　　　11:30 - 14:00
　　　　　18:00 - 21:00
电话:5137766 转 1365

柏香(泸)
新万寿宾馆
营业时间:11:30 - 14:30
　　　　　17:30 - 21:30
电话:4362288 转 2614

步云楼
燕京饭店
营业时间:7:00 - 9:00
　　　　　12:00 - 14:00
　　　　　18:00 - 21:00
电话:8536688 转 16207

绿扬春
新大都饭店
营业时间:11:00 - 14:00
　　　　　17:30 - 21:30
电话:8319988 转 15114

营业时间:11:30 - 14:00
　　　　　17:30 - 21:00
电话:5052288 转 6226

上海餐厅
昆仑饭店
营业时间:11:30 - 14:00
　　　　　17:30 - 21:30
电话:5003388 转 5620

玉兰厅
梅地亚中心
电话:8514422 转 4252

江苏饭店
安定门外大街甘水桥
营业时间:07:00 - 08:00
　　　　　11:30 - 13:30
　　　　　18:00 - 20:00
电话:4226633 转 3705(3859)

湖南菜

曲园酒家　　　　　　　政协文化餐厅
车公庄官园桥　　　　　太平桥大街甲 23 号
营业时间:10:00 - 13:30　营业时间:10:30 - 14:00
　　　　　17:00 - 21:00　　　　　17:00 - 21:30
电话:6062316　　　　　电话:6025758

韶山毛家菜馆
和平里中街甲 4 号
营业时间:10:00 - 14:00
　　　　　16:30 - 21:00
电话:4219340

山西菜

晋阳餐厅　　　　　　　晋阳饭庄
国贸中心　　　　　　　珠市口西大街 241 号
营业时间:10:30 - 13:00　营业时间:10:30 - 14:30
　　　　　17:30 - 21:00　　　　　17:00 - 20:00
电话:5052288 转 8190　电话:3037636

台湾菜

食街　　　　　　　　　青叶
台湾饭店　　　　　　　兆龙饭店
营业时间:9:00 - 22:00　营业时间:11:30 - 14:30
电话:5136688　　　　　　　　　17:30 - 23:30
　　　　　　　　　　　　电话:5002299 转 2102

京叶
新世纪饭店
营业时间:11:30 - 14:00
　　　　　17:30 - 21:30
电话:8491389

美乐啤酒屋
五洲大酒店
营业时间:11:00 - 14:00
　　　　　17:00 - 24:00
电话:4915588 转 72052

野味

豳风堂饭庄
北京动物园
营业时间:10:00 - 14:30
　　　　　16:30 - 21:00
电话:8314411 转 515

蒙古菜

蒙古包
国都茂盛宾酒店
营业时间:18:00 - 22:30
电话:4565588 转 2

晚霞庭
港澳中心
营业时间:18:00 - 23:00
电话:5012288 转 2311

内蒙古风味餐厅
东城区美术馆后街 71 号
营业时间:11:00 - 21:00
特色:拔丝奶豆腐
电话:4014499 转 3337,4043612

北京风味小吃

都一处烧麦馆
前门大街 36 号
电话:5112094

西德顺饭庄
朝阳门内北小街 68 号
电话:4040608

天兴居饭馆　　　　　　锦馨小吃店
崇文区鲜鱼口 95 号　　广渠门外大街 214 号
电话：7023240　　　　　电话：7023690

天地一家春　　　　　　又一顺小吃店
新世纪饭店　　　　　　宣武门内大街 31 号
营业时间：11：30 - 14：00　电话：6036994
　　　　　17：30 - 21：30
电话：8491137

火锅

金火锅　　　　　　　　雅洁餐厅（歪嘴鸡火锅）
新世纪饭店　　　　　　西城区鼓楼东大街 311 号
营业时间：11：00 - 22：00　营业时间：10：30 - 22：00
电话：8491303　　　　　电话：4041015

亚洲渔港火锅厅　　　　皇上皇火锅城
亚洲大酒店　　　　　　海淀区五棵松路口往
　　　　　　　　　　　北 400 米西
营业时间：11：30 - 14：00　营业时间：13：30 - 23：00
　　　　　17：30 - 21：00　特色：精选肥牛
电话：5007788 转 7122　电话：8389278

山釜餐厅海淀分店　　　能人居
（四季火锅）
海淀南路 5 号　　　　　西城区白塔寺 5 号
营业时间：11：00 - 14：00　电话：6012560
　　　　　16：30 - 22：00

电话:2568397,2568396

东来顺饭庄　　　　　　　　　白帝城火锅
王府井大街 198 号　　　　　　宣武区虎坊路 2 号
电话:5253562　　　　　　　　电话:3033491,3187710
东交民巷 44 号　　　　　　　　崇文门西大街 6 号楼
电话:5241042　　　　　　　　电话:5121479
西直门饭店
电话:2257078

怀旧风味

黑土地　　　　　　　　　　　向阳屯食村
和平里东街 9 号　　　　　　　海淀区万泉河路 51 号
电话:4271415　　　　　　　　电话:2562967,2563059

忆苦思甜大杂院　　　　　　　半坡火锅啤酒村
西单北大街辟才胡同 17 号　　王府井大街 26 号
电话:6022640　　　　　　　　电话:5255583

老三届
安定门内大街
电话:4072591

素菜

功德林素菜馆　　　　　　　　北京真斋饭庄
前门南大街 158 号　　　　　　宣武门内大街 74 号
电话:7020867　　　　　　　　电话:6056130

养生斋餐厅　　　　　　时珍苑
西苑饭店　　　　　　　天桥宾馆
营业时间:11:30－14:00　营业时间:11:00－14:00
　　　　　18:00－21:00　　　　　17:30－22:00
电话:8313388 转 10213　电话:3012266

亚洲风味

印度
味美佳餐馆　　　　　　香味廊
亚太大厦餐厅　　　　　金都假日饭店
营业时间:11:00－14:30　营业时间:11:30－14:30
　　　　　18:00－23:30　　　　　18:00－23:30
电话:5139988 转 20188　电话:8322288 转 7107

印度尼西亚
印尼餐厅
丽都假日饭店
营业时间:11:30－14:00
　　　　　18:00－22:00
电话:4376688 转 1847

日本
沙龙餐厅　　　　　　　日本餐厅
北京国际网球中心　　　港澳中心
天坛东路 50 号　　　　营业时间:11:00－14:00
营业时间:10:00－22:00　　　　　17:30－22:00

电话:7012660　　　　　电话:5012288 转 2133

五人百姓
北京饭店
营业时间:11:30 - 14:00
　　　　　17:00 - 20:30
电话:5137766 转 666

银座
王府饭店
营业时间:11:30 - 14:00
　　　　　17:30 - 21:30
电话:5128899 转 7585

安具乐五合庵
天桥宾馆
营业时间:7:00 - 9:00
　　　　　11:00 - 22:00
电话:3012266

白菊厅
梅地亚中心
营业时间:11:30 - 14:00
　　　　　17:00 - 21:00
电话:8514422 转 1738

鸭川
中国大饭店
营业时间:11:30 - 14:30
　　　　　18:00 - 22:00
电话:5052266 转 39

东京
昆仑饭店
营业时间:11:30 - 14:00
　　　　　17:30 - 21:30
电话:5003388 转 5695

京樽料理
首都大酒店
营业时间:11:30 - 14:00
　　　　　17:00 - 21:00
电话:5129988 转 7777

京
新万寿宾馆
营业时间:11:30 - 14:30
　　　　　17:30 - 21:30
电话:4362288 转 2636

源氏
北京希尔顿饭店

樱
长富宫饭店

星期一至六
营业时间:11:30 - 14:00
　　　　　18:00 - 22:00
电话:4662288 转 7402

营业时间:7:00 - 9:00
　　　　　11:30 - 14:00
　　　　　17:30 - 22:00
电话:5125555 转 1226

云海餐厅
新世纪饭店
营业时间:11:30 - 14:00
　　　　　17:00 - 21:30
电话:8491160

三越餐厅
幸福大厦
东三环北路 5 号
营业时间:11:30 - 14:00
　　　　　17:30 - 21:00
电话:4615760

白云
后圆恩寺街 7 号
电话:4034003

朝鲜

萨拉伯尔
亮马大厦
电话:5016688 转 5119
燕莎商城
电话:4651845

北京斗山酒家
南河沿华龙街
营业时间:11:00 - 14:30
　　　　　17:30 - 21:30
电话:5129130

赛特雅里廊
赛特俱乐部
电话:5227502

山釜餐厅
德胜门西大街汇通祠
营业时间:11:00 - 22:00
电话:6014569

韩国餐厅
亚洲锦江大酒店
营业时间:11:30 - 14:00
　　　　　17:30 - 21:00
电话:5007788 转 7038

金龟庄
凯莱大酒店
营业时间:10:30 - 14:00
　　　　　17:30 - 22:00
电话:5158855 转 3255

宝杯苑
北京国际饭店
营业时间:11:30 - 14:30
　　　　　17:30 - 21:30
电话:5129844

京广明月馆
京广中心
营业时间:11:30 - 14:00
　　　　　17:00 - 22:00
电话:5012032

半亚餐厅
东城区美术馆后街 65 号楼
营业时间:11:00 - 14:00
　　　　　17:00 - 21:00
特色:韩国石锅烧烤,
韩式便餐
电话:4031008, 4031006

牡丹峰餐厅
南河沿华龙街
营业时间:10:30 - 14:30
　　　　　17:00 - 21:30
电话:5125133

雪岳山餐厅
新大都饭店
营业时间:11:30 - 14:00
　　　　　17:30 - 21:00
电话:8319988 转 15142

丽德苑(韩)
西苑饭店
电话:8313388

泰国
泰国餐厅

泰国餐厅

丽都假日饭店   松鹤大酒店
营业时间:11:30 - 14:00   营业时间:11:00 - 14:00
          18:00 - 22:00   17:30 - 22:00
电话:4376688 转 2899   电话:5138822 转 2430

越南

西贡苑   芭蕉别墅
凯莱大酒店   昆仑饭店
营业时间:11:30 - 14:00   营业时间:11:30 - 14:00
          17:30 - 22:00   17:30 - 21:30
电话:5158855   电话:5003388 转 5247

西餐

王朝   旋转餐厅
京伦饭店   昆仑饭店
营业时间:7:00 - 9:30   营业时间:6:30 - 9:30
          11:30 - 14:00   12:00 - 14:00
          18:00 - 22:30   18:00 - 23:30
电话:5002266 转 53   电话:5003388 转 5507

橄榄绿   兰花台
新万寿宾馆   长富宫饭店
营业时间:24 小时   营业时间:5:30 - 24:00
电话:4362288 转 2617   电话:5125555 转 1036

莫斯科餐厅(俄)   茂盛宾餐厅
西外大街 135 号   国都茂盛宾饭店

营业时间:11:00-13:30　　营业时间:6:00-23:30
　　　　　16:30-22:00　　电话:4565588 转 2
电话:8316677-4331

玫瑰厅(俄)　　　　　　　幸运阁
梅地亚中心　　　　　　　赛特饭店
营业时间:6:00-24:00　　营业时间:24 小时
电话:8514422 转 5　　　电话:5123388 转 2234

长富宫西餐厅　　　　　　皇都扒房
营业时间:11:30-14:00　　粤海皇都酒店
　　　　　17:30-22:00　　营业时间:14:00-22:30
电话:5125555 转 1225　　电话:5136666

阿波罗咖啡厅　　　　　　新大都西餐厅
兆龙饭店　　　　　　　　新大都饭店
营业时间:7:30-24:00　　营业时间:18:00-01:00
电话:5002299　　　　　　电话:8319988 转 15121

棕榈园　　　　　　　　　紫门
王府饭店　　　　　　　　国际艺苑
营业时间:5:30-10:00　　皇冠假日饭店
　　　　　11:30-14:30　　营业时间:12:00-14:00
　　　　　18:00-24:00　　　　　　18:30-22:00
电话:5128899 转 7561　　电话:5133388 转 1130

建国咖啡厅　　　　　　　共享咖啡厅
建国饭店　　　　　　　　皇冠假日饭店

营业时间:6:00-24:00　　营业时间:6:30-23:30
电话:5002233　　　　　　电话:5133388 转 1102

凯莱咖啡厅　　　　　　　红墙咖啡厅
凯莱大酒店　　　　　　　贵宾楼饭店
营业时间:6:30-23:30　　营业时间:7:00-24:00
电话:5158855　　　　　　电话:5137788 转 343

露台咖啡厅　　　　　　　欧陆餐厅
天坛饭店　　　　　　　　北京饭店
营业时间:6:30-21:30　　营业时间:11:30-14:00
电话:7012277 转 2120　　　　　　　18:00-20:30
　　　　　　　　　　　　电话:5137766 转 1384

京广中心　　　　　　　　怡时厅
营业时间:6:30-14:30　　凯宾斯基饭店
　　　　　18:30-21:30　营业时间:7:00-24:00
电话:5018888 转 2513　　电话:4653388 转 4105

咖啡苑　　　　　　　　　沁园咖啡厅
中国大饭店　　　　　　　丽都假日饭店
营业时间:24 小时　　　　营业时间:24 小时
电话:5052266 转 35　　　电话:4376688 转 1971

客来思乐餐厅　　　　　　三江咖啡厅
燕莎中心　　　　　　　　国贸饭店
营业时间:11:00-24:00　营业时间:6:00-22:30
电话:4653388　　　　　　电话:5052277 转 35

美国

路易斯安娜
北京希尔顿酒店
每星期一至六
营业时间:11:30－14:00
　　　　　18:00－22:00
电话:4662288 转 7420

云海餐厅
中国大饭店
营业时间:11:30－14:30
　　　　　18:00－22:00
电话:5052266 转 6549

德克萨斯扒房
丽都假日饭店
营业时间:11:30－14:00
　　　　　17:30－23:00
电话:4376688 转 1849

天外天
北京展览馆宾馆
营业时间:7:00－24:00
电话:8316633 转 7011

英国

乡村酒吧
朝阳区三里屯友谊餐厅
营业时间:14:30－24:00
电话:5323063

法国

百花
中国大饭店
营业时间:11:30－14:30
　　　　　18:00－22:30
电话:5052266 转 6697

沙巴里餐厅
北京香格里拉饭店
营业时间:12:00－14:30
　　　　　18:00－22:30
电话:8412211 转 2719

马克西姆餐厅
崇文门西大街 2 号
营业时间:11:00－20:30
电话:5121992

凯旋门西餐厅
王府井大街甲 27 号
营业时间:10:30－24:30
电话:5254918

梅林
兆龙饭店
营业时间:11:30－14:00
　　　　　18:00－22:00
电话:5002299 转 2302

法国餐厅
长城饭店
营业时间:11:45－14:00
　　　　　18:00－22:00
电话:5005566 转 2119

建国西餐厅
建国饭店
营业时间:6:30－9:30
　　　　　12:00－14:00
　　　　　18:00－22:30
电话:5002233 转 8039

德国

德国餐厅
丽都假日饭店
营业时间:17:30－23:30
电话:4376688 转 3815

布诺斯酒吧
中国大饭店
营业时间:11:00－02:00
电话:5052266 转 6565

巴伐利亚啤酒屋
王府饭店
营业时间:12:00－22:30

啤酒坊
凯宾斯基饭店
营业时间:11:30－24:30

电话:5128899 转 7410　　　电话:4653388 转 5732

豪夫门啤酒坊　　　　　　　欣欣大酒店
东三环北路 15 号　　　　　　西单北大街 6 号
电话:5914598　　　　　　　电话:6078830

莫扎特餐厅
凯宾斯基饭店
营业时间:12:00 - 14:00
　　　　　18:00 - 22:00
电话:4653388 转 4156

意大利
帕皮诺　　　　　　　　　　意大利餐厅
北京香格里拉饭店　　　　　丽都假日饭店
营业时间:18:00 - 22:30　　营业时间:11:30 - 24:30
电话:8412211 转 2727　　　电话:4376688 转 3812

罗马餐厅　　　　　　　　　图拉餐厅
王府饭店　　　　　　　　　国际饭店
营业时间:11:30 - 14:30　　营业时间:12:00 - 14:00
　　　　　18:30 - 23:00　　　　　　18:30 - 22:00
电话:5128899 转 7492　　　电话:5129962

威尼斯餐厅　　　　　　　　濠江扒房
凯宾斯基饭店　　　　　　　港澳中心瑞士酒店
营业时间:11:30 - 14:00　　营业时间:11:30 - 14:00
　　　　　17:30 - 23:00　　　　　　18:00 - 22:00

电话:4653388 转 5707　　　电话:5012288 转 2271

新侨西餐厅
新侨饭店
营业时间:7:00 – 23:00
电话:5133366 转 1618

墨西哥
阿尔弗雷德
粤海皇都酒店
营业时间:17:30 – 02:00
电话:5136666 转 2133

北欧
北欧扒房　　　　　　　　皇室咖啡座
北京皇家萨斯大饭店　　　北京皇家萨斯大饭店
营业时间:18:30 – 22:00　营业时间:6:00 – 01:00
电话:4663388 转 3420　　电话:4663388

瑞士
瑞士餐厅　　　　　　　　瑞士咖啡厅
国都茂盛宾饭店　　　　　港澳中心
营业时间:18:00 – 22:30　营业时间:24 小时
电话:4565588 转 2　　　电话:5012288 转 2127

快餐
加州牛肉面大王　　　　　丽都快餐城
东四西大街 26 号　　　　前门西大街正阳市场 1 号

亚太大厦二楼
营业时间:8:00－22:00

营业时间:9:00－22:00
电话:3034243

毕胜客
东直门外大街 27 号,
友谊商店一层
营业时间:9:00－21:30

肯德基家乡鸡
前门,
东四
营业时间:9:00－21:30

国贸大厦美味居快餐城
国贸地下一层
营业时间:11:00－21:00

电话:5052288 转 6180

北京麦当劳餐厅
东长安街甲 31 号
复兴门长安商场,展览路,
东大桥
营业时间:8:30－23:00

山姆叔叔快餐厅
建国门外大街 24 号
营业时间:7:30－22:00
电话:5158833

燕莎快餐厅
燕莎中心西楼
营业时间:7:00－21:00
电话:4653388

比诺比萨饼屋
昆仑饭店西侧
营业时间:9:00－22:00
电话:5003388

茶室中国大饭店
营业时间:9:00－21:00

游乐场所

北京游乐园

位于市东南崇文区龙潭湖公园内,面积 18 公顷,有过山车、海盗船、观览车等若干游乐项目。

公共汽车:6、12、41、64

开放时间:9:00 - 18:00

石景山游乐园

位于城西石景山区八角街,有 40 多个游乐项目,有水上世界、原子滑车等。

公共汽车:337、307、地铁

开放时间:9:00 - 16:45

九龙游乐园

位于城西北十三陵水库。是亚洲最大的水下游乐园。利用声光电技术展现中国古代故事,有目前北京规模最大的水族馆。

公共汽车:912

开放时间:8:00 - 16:30

密云国际游乐园

位于城东北密云县内,距市中心 27 公里,有 20 个游乐项目,有水上舞厅、游艺室等。

开放时间:8:30 - 16:30

文艺演出

作为中国的文化中心，北京集中了全国一流的文艺团体，拥有众多国际国内享有盛誉的艺术家。京剧、芭蕾、杂技、交响乐，传统的民间表演艺术活跃的省、市间、国际间的文化交流使北京的舞台异彩纷呈，具有浓郁的民族特色。在北京，观赏各种艺术表演是不容错过的享受。

在北京可以观赏到的艺术品种有：

京剧

有近 200 年历史，流行全国，是最具有民族代表性的剧种，在世界艺术宝库中也占有重要地位。京剧有优美、独特的唱腔和舞蹈，并融入了中国武术的技巧。演唱讲究，行腔吐字、念白具有音乐性。角色根据男、女、老、少、俊、丑、正、邪，分为生、旦、净、丑四大行当。还有让人称奇的脸谱和辉煌艳丽的服装头饰，一套戏装常常就是珍贵的艺术品。

昆曲

昆曲已有 500 年历史，继承了中国古典诗词、骈文、平话的传统，具有很高的文学性，有大量题材广泛、久为流传的剧目。

昆曲的唱腔悠扬典雅，有近千支南北曲牌，表演丰富细腻、舞蹈优美含蓄。

评剧

　　起源于中国北方民间说唱"莲花落"和民间歌舞"蹦蹦儿戏",具有浓郁的生活气息,唱词通俗易懂,富于叙述性、唱腔口语化,吐字清晰,善于表现平民百姓的生活,深受北京市民喜爱。

河北梆子

　　流传于天津、北京、河北一带的地方戏曲。河北梆子有很多剧目,它的演唱高亢激越、刚劲有力,善于表达慷慨悲壮的情绪。表演上以唱功见长。

曲艺

　　京味最浓的艺术形式,有相声、大鼓、单弦等,是由民间艺人的表演发展而来。

木偶戏

　　木偶戏在中国已有 2000 年历史。它综合了戏剧、歌舞、音乐、绘画、雕刻等艺术手法,在表演上具有生动、夸张、灵活的艺术特点。

杂技

　　激动人心的杂技表演是各国朋友喜爱的艺术。

歌剧

　　在北京可以欣赏到大型歌剧。

节日民俗

春节

　　春节中国农历新年,一般在每年公历二月间。在北京,春节的传统色彩最为浓厚。节日气氛从节前半个月就开始了,商店张灯结彩,延长营业时间,供应大量年货。1993 年,北京市人民政府正式颁布了禁放烟花爆竹的法规,使放鞭炮这一传统习俗成为历史。

　　春节有三天假期,不少人家用彩带、灯笼装饰房间,郊区农户必要贴春联、剪窗花。家家要筹办年货和准备给亲友拜年的礼品。除夕之夜,全家团圆,包饺子,吃年夜饭、欢乐通宵。

　　花会、庙会、灯会是春节至元宵节期间举行的隆重的民俗活动。场面宏大、热闹非凡,各种民间歌舞器乐,说唱表演和红火热闹的年货市场,是北京市民节日必游之处,也吸引着回乡的港澳、台湾同胞和各国来客。

元旦

　　元旦有两天假期,人们常用来探亲访友。

中秋节

　　北京人把中秋节作为第二大传统节日,是家人团聚、共叙天伦的日子。中秋节必须吃月饼,市场上出售京式、广式、苏式月饼。

国庆节

法定节日中最隆重的是国庆节。国庆期间北京最漂亮,天安门广场和主要街道两侧装饰着鲜花、国旗、彩旗。国庆节当天,北京各大公园免费开放。

大钟寺辞旧迎新"元旦"敲钟晚会

每年元旦和农历春节,北三环西路的大钟寺都举办敲钟活动,这里的永乐大钟,音色美妙,这两个年节的除夕之夜,许多人都想听到它洪亮壮阔的声音,这里特地为国内外游人举办敲钟晚会。春节期间,初一到初三的早、午、晚,各鸣钟一次,并举办文化庙会。

龙庆峡冰灯艺术节

在北郊延庆县风光幽美的龙庆峡,每年冬季,都举办大型冰灯艺术节,这里气温比北京市区低,结冰早,化冰迟,为制作冰雕提供了条件,晶莹洁白的各式造型的冰雕中,装上了五彩缤纷的电灯,如同步入童话世界。

迎春庙会、花会

每年春节期间,北京地区在多处举办的传统庙会、花会,吸引大量游人,主要有地坛文化庙会、白云观民俗庙会、龙潭湖大型花会等。

庙会原是寺庙借一个宗教节日,在庙内烧香礼佛,因香客多,各色货摊、饮食摊、杂耍等纷纷赶来,有吃的、看的,还可买点纪念品,形成一种群众性游乐活动。

所谓花会,是北京郊区农村利用农闲时期自办的游艺表演,如舞龙、耍狮、踩高跷、跑旱船、跑驴和打太平鼓等,很受农民欢迎。近年郊区各地每年春节也办花会,有时还到颐和园等处表演。

大观园迎春会

北京大观园在春节期间办迎春会,园内有以《红楼梦》题材的演出和猜灯谜等活动,备有红楼古装供游人穿戴拍照。最引人注目的是"元妃省亲"表演,100多人身穿华丽古装,装扮为仪仗队,护拥"元妃"官轿入园,浩浩荡荡,再现书中所描述的盛况。

元宵灯会

过去每年从正月初六至十七日,在厂甸等处有灯会,除去各种花灯、走马灯以外,还猜灯谜。现在用电照明,有机械传动,灯会更加丰富,五光十色,绚丽夺目。近年劳动人民文化宫每年都有灯会,圆明园、紫竹院也举办科技灯会。特别是北海公园的冰灯,延庆龙庆峡的冰灯展,造型多样,并有民间故事题材,五彩缤纷、晶莹玉洁,游人如织。

大愿法会

在北京最大的喇嘛庙雍和宫,每年都举行盛大的大愿法会,全体喇嘛要诵经祈祷吉祥,并进行跳布扎(俗称打鬼)表演。

赏花活动

春节前后,中山公园的兰花展。春季,北京植物园的桃花节,各公园的牡丹、月季花展,玉渊潭公园的

樱花,颐和园的玉兰花,妙峰山玫瑰。秋季,各公园的
菊花展等。有很多人前往赏花。

风筝赛

北京放风筝历史悠久,人们在春、秋有放风筝爱
好,北京地区的风筝有 5 类形式和多种流派。近年清
明节在门头沟区举办"国际风筝会",每年都有不少国
家和地区的风筝爱好者前来参赛。各式风筝竞相飞
翔,很多观众前往参观。

龙舟竞赛

每年农历端午节前后,颐和园、龙潭湖有划龙舟
比赛,全国各地派代表队参赛,届时锣鼓喧天,岸上欢
声不绝,情绪热烈。

西瓜节

京郊大兴县盛产西瓜,名优品种很多,盛夏瓜熟
季节举办西瓜节,备有优质西瓜供游人品尝、购买。

夏季消夏灯会

市区北海公园,西北郊圆明园遗址公园,举办过
几届灯会,利用现代化设备,制作各式彩灯,入夜流金
溢彩,妙景纷呈,吸引了大量游人。

颐和园昆明湖夜游

颐和园辽阔的昆明湖上,夏季夜晚乘龙舟,游湖
观景,上岸散步,都很惬意。末代皇帝踪迹游

北京后海原醇王府(现在是宋庆龄故居)是溥仪

的出生地,故宫是溥仪当皇帝时住过的地方,附近的清东陵、西陵有清王朝陵墓群,还有溥仪被特赦后在北京工作、居住过的地方及其亲友住所。这些地方有些已对外开放。

中秋赏月晚会

农历八月十五日,是中国传统的中秋节,颐和园苏州街,复兴门外的月坛公园,以及一些宾馆、饭店,都举办中秋赏月晚会,有时北京天文馆等处,也办观月活动。

重阳游山会

农历九月初九,是九九重阳节,人们有重阳登高的秋游习惯。北京西郊八大处风景区,每年举办游山会,其他公园也举办类似活动。

香山红叶节

西郊香山公园有大片红叶林,每年霜降前后,9万多株黄栌树叶和枫树叶,红林如火似锦,极为壮观,成为人们秋游胜地。其他有红叶林的风景区,也吸引很多游人。

北京文物节

近年北京文物部门开始举办文物节,在主会场(文化宫)举办文物展,各文博馆所,也同时展出文物精品,以展示珍藏文物。

第四章　工作在北京

商务联络

　　北京得天独厚的政治条件,丰富的资源以及它所具备的比较完善的交通、电讯、市政基础设施,门类齐全的工业基础和人才优势,使它在吸收外资方面始终是最具竞争力的城市之一,对于商务人员和投资者来说,北京充满着机会和成功的梦想,目前中国正在迈向社会主义市场经济,与北京做生意正值黄金时机。

工作时间和假期

　　办公时间通常是早上 8 点至下午 5 点。中午有大约 1 至 2 小时午餐时间。每周工作五天,星期六、日为休息日。

　　法定假期是春节 3 天,国庆节 2 天,五一国际劳动节 1 天,元旦节 1 天,其余则正常上班。

商务中心

　　饭店内都有商务中心,24 小时营业,有会多种语言的工作人员,办公设备包括电脑、复印机和传真机等。(打字机等也可租用),还有邮政、快递,提供小型会议室和会议设备等服务。租金不等,预先商定。

位于京广中心的宏宇商务中心及燕莎中心的雷格斯商务中心提供设施完备的出租办公室。短期在京或经常往返的商务客人可随时租用,并可提供规范的秘书服务,代客人接收信件等。

会议及展览中心
北京国际会议中心

位于亚运村,可举行各种不同规格的会议、展览、贸易会、时装表演等。有 2 个大厅。大会议厅能容纳 2,800 人,小的能容纳 600 人。展览中心有 4 个标准的展厅,面积约 5,500 平方米。另有 48 个较小的艺术厅、会议室、演说厅,其中一个 48 座位的会议厅有 6 种语言的同声翻译。运动员餐厅可同时接待 2500 人。电话:4993575

中国国际贸易中心

国际贸易中心内有与饭店、办公楼相连的会议和展览中心。拥有先进通讯设备的会议大厅,能接待 2,000 余人,在里面可举行招待会或舞台表演。另外还有能容纳 1,100 人的剧院,850 人的宴会厅和 38 个接待从 10 人到 380 人不等的多功能厅。展览中心分为两层,面积达 7,378 平方米。有直接的汽车通道。两层展厅分别为 3,470 平方米、高 4.3 米和 2,090 平方米、高 2.9 米,另有一个 1,818 平方米的装货厅,高度为 19 米。电话:5052266

中国国际展览中心

位于北三环路，拥有中国最大的展览设施，面积为 17 万平方米。电话：4664433

二十一世纪饭店中日青年交流中心

位于朝阳区亮马河路，有剧院、语言训练中心、会议厅、研究楼等。电话：4663311

梅地亚中心

是中央电视台（CCTV）和日本广播协会（NHK）共同合作兴建的，集电视节目制作、卫星传送、宾馆、公寓、写字楼服务设施于一体的综合性企业，位于北京交通主干线——西长安街北侧，紧临中央电视台和风景秀丽的玉渊潭公园。

外商投资审批、管理和服务部门

外商投资审批、管理和服务机构接受中外投资者的委托，提供设立外商投资企业的咨询服务，介绍投资机会和合作伙伴及提供市场调研。为中外投资者和外商投资企提供涉外经济法律顾问。为中外投资者代拟和修改项目建议书、可行性研究报告、合同、章程以及其它商务文件。为外国公司代办在北京设立办事处的全部申报手续。而北京外国企业服务总公司为海外企业驻京代表机构提供中方工作人员及相关的服务。

由北京市政府新闻办公室、北京市经贸委、北京市计委合办的"北京月讯"商务特刊,介绍北京市最新的投资政策、投资环境等,在各大宾馆免费取阅。

北京市外商投资服务中心

北京市外商投资服务中心(以下简称"中心")是北京市外商投资管理委员会常设办事机构和北京外商投资企业协会常设办事机构,同时也是北京市外资企业的主管部门。

"中心"是政府部门与外商投资企业之间联系的桥梁和纽带。"中心"的宗旨是:服务中外投资者、服务外商投资企业、服务首都经济建设。"中心"的方针是:改善投资环境、发挥窗口功能、提供系统服务、热情周到迅捷。"中心"主要设有联络部、信息部、咨询部、企业管理部、法律事务部,拥有一批熟悉涉外经济法规、熟悉草拟涉外经济法律文件、依法处理涉外经济纠纷的专业人才,维护了中外投资者和外商投资企业的正当权益。

"中心"的主要业务是:

一、接受中外投资者的委托,提供设立外商投资企业的咨询服务,介绍投资机会和合作伙伴。

二、接受中外投资者的委托,代拟和修改项目建议书、可行性研究报告、合同、章程以及其他商务法律文件,并代办全部申报手续。

三、为境外公司代办在北京设立办事处的全部申报手续。

四、接受委托,为境外公司、企业和其他经济组织进行行业、市场投资意向、资信专题或综合的调研。

五、"中心"是在京外资企业的主管部门,承担外资企业的中国职工人事档案管理、办理出国手续、职称评定。承办外资企业办公用房、职工住户申报手续、保险等管理及服务工作。

六、组织国内外涉外经济、技术交流、项目招商活动。组织外商投资企业参加国内外经济洽谈会、研讨会、展览会、交易会、展销会等。

七、组织北京市区、县、局(总公司、集团公司)外经干部审批外商投资企业法律文件的培训和资格审定,组织对北京市外商投资企业中方高级管理人员和各类专业人员的培训工作。

八、应聘担任外商投资企业常年法律顾问,接受委托协调解决外商投资企业的法律纠纷,承办外商投资企业特别清算。

九、编制北京市利用外资工作对外宣传资料,编制和提供外商投资法规汇编等其他资料。

地址:北京市海淀区北三环中路 31 号凯奇大厦七层

邮编:100088

电话:2023332 - 2708,2702,2710,2109
　　　　2023332 - 2703

北京市投资咨询服务中心

北京市投资咨询服务中心(以下简称"中心")以市政府研究室和市计划委员会为主,吸引有关部门参加选派精干人员组成,是沟通本市经济组织与国内外投资者、合作者联系的中介服务机构。它将为客商在京从事经济活动,提供便捷、准确、完善、周到的服务。

主要业务:

储备备选项目,积极为投资者寻找投资机会。

为投资者提供投资政策、申报程序、建设条件等多方面的咨询服务。

以多种形式向国内外发布招商信息,组织招商活动,培训招商谈判人才。

承接市场商情调查和项目可行性研究。

代办投资项目申报批准手续。并受市政府有关部门委托组织"全程一站"式的审批服务。

承接国内外投资者和市内经济组织委托的其它事项,在规定范围内从事商务活动。

地址:北京市西城区百万庄大街东路甲2号

邮编:100037

电话:8315349,8315343

中国国际贸易促进委员会北京市分会

中国国际贸易促进委员会北京市分会亦称北京国际商会,是由北京市经济贸易界有代表性的人士、企业和团体组成的,在北京有一定实力和影响的民间国际经贸组织。其宗旨是:积极开展促进对外贸易,利用外资,引进先进技术设备和各种形式的中外经济技术合作等活动,促进北京地区同世界各国,各地区之间的贸易和经济关系的发展。

主要业务:

一、与国际商会、各国工商会和其他国际经济贸易组织、工商团体及其驻京机构联络,参加其举办的有关活动;组织或同国外相应机构合办有关经济贸易方面的国际会议;邀请和接待国外经济贸易、技术界代表团(组)和人士来京访问、考察;组织北京市经济贸易、技术代表团(组)出国访问考察;接待、承办中外贸易洽谈会、技术交流会和国外新产品样品、样本陈列会。

二、为国内外有关企业和经济机构提供贸易和经济技术合作等方面信息,开办北京地区国际经贸信息服务网,寻找贸易机会,介绍合资、合作对象。

三、同世界各国、各地区的博(展)览会组织联络,组织北京对外经济贸易企业团体在国外举办经济贸易展览(销)会或参加博览会,主办或承办国外和台、港、澳地区在京举办经济贸易与技术展览会,并提供有关服务。

四、为国内外经济贸易企业和组织提供有关国际经贸、投资、技术转让等方面的法律咨询服务;为企业担任法律顾问;开办"中国贸促会首都调解中心",调解涉外经济贸易纠纷;出具北京出口商品原产地证明书,签发和认证对外贸易和货物运输业务的文件与单证。

五、接受委托,承办经贸业务代理和出口商品商标注册申请的代理工作,承办项目可行性调查和评估,协助企业谈判和签约以及提供企业管理、财会、审计等方面的咨询服务。

六、联合北京市对外贸易进出口公司、重点工商企业组织,主办"北京世界贸易中心",沟通与世界各地世界贸易中心协会会员间的相互了解与合作,传递经济贸易信息,提供有关服务。

地址:北京市东城区南河沿华龙街中楼二段四层
邮编:100006
电话:5125175

传真:(010)5125165

与商务服务有关的机构

外商投资企业审批、管理和服务部门

北京市对外经济贸易委员会 北京市经济委员会
地址:朝阳门内大街190号 地址:正义路2号
电话:5137733   电话:5193323

北京市计划委员会   北京市商业委员会
地址:百万庄大街东路甲2号 地址:正义路2号
电话:8311680   电话:5192619

北京市市政管理委员会   北京市政府农林办公室
地址:正义路2号   地址:台基厂3号
电话:3088467   电话:3088114

北京市城乡建设委员会   北京市城市规划管理局
地址:南礼士路头条3号 地址:西城区南礼士路60号
电话:8526754   电话:8522994

北京市工商行政管理局   北京市税务局对外税务分局
电话:3469955   地址:工体北路新中街13号
外商投资登记处   电话:4660568,4670631
电话:3494310

北京市财政局   国家外汇管理局北京分局
地址:海淀区阜成路15号 地址:月坛南街79号

电话:8423355 8125355　　电话:8572108

北京市物价局　　　　　北京市房地产管理局
地址:崇文区兴隆街 51 号　地址:南河沿大街南湾子
　　　　　　　　　　　胡同 1 号
电话:7013564　　　　　电话:5124104

北京海关　　　　　　　北京市房屋土地管理局
地址:建国门内大街 6 号　地址:崇文区天坛公园东门
电话:5194416　　　　　电话:7013326

北京进出口商品检验局　北京市统计局
地址:建国门外大街 12 号　地址:宣武区槐柏树街 2 号
电话:5004860　　　　　电话:3021067

北京市劳动局　　　　　北京市外商投资服务中心
地址:宣武区槐柏树街 2 号　地址:北三环东路凯奇楼 7/F
电话:3021377　　　　　电话:2023332 转 2707 或
　　　　　　　　　　　2704

北京投资咨询服务中心　北京外国企业服务总公司
地址:百万庄东大街 2 号　地址:朝阳门南大街 14 号
电话:8315349　　　　　电话:5016677

出入境
北京市人民政府外事　　北京市公安局外国人
办公室护照签证处　　　出入境管理处
地址:正义路 2 号　　　地址:北池子大街 85 号

电话:5192881

电话:5255486

北京市公安局中国公
民出入境管理处
地址:东交民巷 38 号
电话:5241440

北京对外联络事务咨
询服务中心
地址:朝阳门内大街 190 号
电话:5257829 或 5137210

通讯服务

北京市内电话局
东单营业厅

北京无线通讯局营业厅
地址:西直门内后半壁店
街 56 号

地址:建国门内大街 65 号
电话:5124559
西单营业厅
地址:西单北大街 131 号
电话:6021511

电话:6050311 或 3011333

北京国际电信之窗
地址:东三环北路 5 号
电话:5008000

北京长途电话局营业大厅
地址:复兴门内大街 97 号
电话:6022969

北京电信综合业务营业中心
地址:国贸大厦 B1
电话:5051000 或 5321000

北京国际邮局
地址:建国门北大街
电话:5128120

交通运输

机场问讯
电话:4563604

外企航空服务公司
地址:国贸大厦 1 楼

电话:5053330

民航营业大厦
地址:西长安街 15 号
电话:6017755
国内机票预订
电话:6013336
国际机票预订
电话:6016667

火车站问询处

电话:5633622

机票预订
电话:5052258 或 5052259

北京市出租汽车管理局
电话:6012620

中国民航客货代理公司
地址:三里屯东兴路 8 号
电话:4665370 或 4665371

鸿运国际运输服务有限公司
地址:安定门外小关皇姑
坟 1 号
电话:4260886 转 889 或 881

中国航空服务有限公司
地址:朝外大街 225 号
电话:5065533

中外运北京公司

海运电话:4652354
铁路货运电话:3814440 转 211
航空货运电话:5011041
展览运输电话:4671713
汽车运输电话:3813378

金融服务机构
中国银行北京市分行
地址:东安门大街 19 号
电话:5199416

中国工商银行北京市分行
地址:白云路 10 号
电话:3013101

中国人民银行北京市分行　中国人民建设银行
　　　　　　　　　　　　北京市分行
地址:前门西河沿 9 号　　地址:广安门外马连道
　　　　　　　　　　　　北路 1 号
电话:3035254, 5199437　电话:3265301

国家外汇管理局北京分局　中国农业银行北京市分行
外汇调剂中心
地址:月坛南街 9 号　　　地址:天坛东门水道子
　　　　　　　　　　　　胡同 15 号
电话:8572108　　　　　　电话:7014233

交通银行北京市分行　　　中信实业银行
地址:崇文区天坛东里　　地址:新源南路 6 号
北区 12 号
电话:7016528, 7016529　电话:5122233

法律服务

北京市司法局　　　　　　北京市公证处
地址:永定门外　　　　　　电话:5019664
电话:7212227

北京市对外经济律师事务所　中国环球律师事务所
地址:劳动人民文化宫　　地址:北三环东路 SAS 皇
　　　　　　　　　　　　家饭店 3/F
电话:5133167, 5133168　电话:4652315

北京天平律师事务所　　　中国法律咨询中心

地址:王府井大街 20 号　地址:王府井大街 20 号
电话:5135261　　　　　电话:5135261

快递及搬迁服务
中外运－－敦豪国际航空　中外运－－天地快件
快件有限公司　　　　　有限公司
地址:朝阳区新源街 45 号　地址:曙光西里 14 楼
电话:4662211　　　　　电 话: 4677877（递 送）
　　　　　　　　　　　4672517(询问)

联合包裹运输公司　　　宅急送
地址:安定路 12 号　　　地址:农展馆南路 9 号
电话:4651565　　　　　电 话: 5084775, 5067719,
　　　　　　　　　　　5084775

北京邮政速递局　　　　嘉佰(中国)有限公司
地址:前门东大街 7 号　地址:中信大厦 1104 室
电话:5129947, 5129948　电话:5002255 转 1140

商务大厦
国贸大厦　　　　　　　国际大厦
地址:建国门外大街 1 号　地址:建国门外大街 15 号
电话:5052288　　　　　电话:5002255

京广中心　　　　　　　京城大厦
地址:朝阳区呼家楼　　　地址:新源南路 6 号
电话:5013388　　　　　电话:4660088

燕莎中心
地址:亮马桥路 50 号
电话:4653388

赛特大厦
地址:建国门外大街 22 号
电话:5122288

亚太大厦
地址:朝阳区雅宝路 8 号
电话:5139988

汇宾大厦
地址:北辰东路 8 号
电话:4993886

发展大厦
地址:东三环北路 5 号
电话:5018811

幸福大厦
地址:东三环北路 3 号
电话:4615760

展览馆、会议中心

中国国际展览中心
地址:朝阳区北三环东路 6 号
电话:4664433

北京国际会议中心
地址:亚运村
电话:4993571

国贸中心展览大厅
地址:建国门外大街 1 号
电话:5053832

北京笔克展览服务有限公司
地址:安慧里 3 区
电话:4916592

北京展览馆
地址:西直门外大街 135 号
电话:8323551

北京梅地亚中心
地址:复兴路 11 号 B
电话:8514422

中日青年交流中心
地址:亮马桥路 40 号
电话:4663311

附录：常用电话

国内长途人工挂号台	113
国内长途半自动挂号台	173
北京远郊长途挂号台	118
国际长途挂号台	115
国内长途查询台	116
国内长途查号台	174
电话查号台	114
天气预报台	121
电话报时台	117
北京火车站问询处	5128931
首都汽车公司	4616688
旅游汽车公司	5158604
北京市出租汽车公司	8322561
北京海关	5194114
北京市公安局外国人员 管理、出入境管理处	5255486
中国国际航空公司	5129525
国内电话定座	4014441
国际电话定座	4012221
售票服务处总机	4013331
首都机场问询处	4563604

北京急用电话

火警	119 或 6030224
匪警	110
北京急救中心	120

	5255678
石景山区急救站	8878956
东城区急救站	4034567
宣武区急救站	3464406
朝阳区急救站	5024214
海淀区急救站	2551759
丰台区急救站	3823477

CONTENTS

Chapter 1 COME TO BEIJING

ABOUT BEIJING

To many foreign visitors, Beijing is an enormous treasure house of cultural and historical relics, stocked with various collections of palaces, temples, parks and above all, one of the seven wonders of the world, the Great Wall. It is a mysterious land with a striking contrast between the numerous traces of old tradition and the modern metropolitan life. Beijing of the 1990s has the best of many things in China — the best roads, the best transport and communication, the best restaurants and hotels. . . . Yet what impresses visitors most is its long history and rich culture. Beijing was the ruling center of China for several kingdoms and dynasties, and it has remained to be the center of China's political and cultural life in addition to its role as a major trading center and a place of strategic importance. If you share the view that one cannot know the Orient without visiting China, you would also agree that one cannot know China without visiting Beijing. Tourists, especially those who come with a tour group, often leave the city with overcrowded memories because they would have seen too many things in too short a time. Yes, it is hard to pick up at random a few places of interest from its dozens of urban and suburban sights to be acquainted with its history or to taste a few dishes to appreciate its culinary delights.

Location

Beijing is located in the southern part of the North China Plain. The city center is situated at Latitude 39°6'N and Longitude 116°20'E. It is surrounded by mountains of the Taihang and Yanshan ranges in the west, north and northeast, with the broad plain to the southeast.

City Flowers: Chinese rose and chrysanthemum

City Trees: Oriental Arborvitae and Cypress

Topography

Beijing covers an area of 16,808 square kilometers. Of the total, urban areas account for 750 square kilometers. The Taihang and Yanshan mountain ranges taper off to the northwestern part of the city. The southeastern part is a plain tilting toward the Bohai Sea. Hilly regions take up 62 percent of the city's total area. Five rivers of Yongding, Chaobai, Juma, Juhe and North Grand Canal run by the city and pour into the Bohai Sea.

The city center is 43.71 meters above sea level. The mountains average from 1,000 to 1,500 meters above sea level, with the highest Lingshan Peak measuring 2,303 meters, whereas the nadir point is less than ten meters above sea level.

History

Beijing is the capital of the People's Republic of China, and China's political and cultural center. Beijing is one of the historical and cultural cities and ancient capitals of the world. As early as 700,000 years ago, the primitive tribe, Peking Man, appeared in the Zhoukoudian area of

Beijing. In its earliest recorded history, Beijing was called
Ji, the capital of the princedom of Jin. From 221 B. C. ,
when Emperor Qin Shihuang united China, to 937 A. D. ,
Beijing was a place of strategic importance and the capital
of several northern kingdoms. In 938 A. D. , Beijing
(named Yanjing then) became the secondary capital of
the Liao Dynasty, which ruled over northern China.
Within the ensuing 650 years, Beijing was the capital of
the Jin, Yuan, Ming and Qing dynasties. On October 1,
1949, upon the founding of the People's Republic of China, Beijing became the national capital.

Population

Beijing has a population of over 10 million, among
which urban dwellers amount to 73. 1 percent. With an
influx of over 3 million Chinese provincials, downtown
Beijing is always alive with people.

Ethnic Groups & Religion

Each of China's 56 ethnic groups has its permanent
residents in Beijing. The Han accounts for 96. 2 percent
of the total. The 55 other ethnic minorities combine to
count 300, 000 people, of which the Hui (Muslims),
Manchu and Mongolian take the top three places. Among
them 210,000 are Hui (Muslims).

Buddhism was the most influential religion among
the Beijingers. This could easily be seen from the large
numbers of temples built in the city and the large scale
renovation work carried out through various dynasties.
These temples contain precious cultural relics and masterpieces of works of art which made them both as places of
worship and popular historical sights.

Islamism is the religion for the Hui people. The Niujie Mosque and Dongsi Mosque both have a history of five
hundred years. Catholicism was introduced to Beijing in

the late years of the Ming Dynasty. The oldest Cathedral Nantang still remains intact. Protestantism did not make the same impact on Beijing as Catholicism. But many of the churches and societies established by missionaries still exist. Religious activities have revived since the late 1970s. Today in Beijing, regular services are held for all these religions. Believers of the younger generation are taking a great interest in studying the basics of the religion in addition to attending services.

Administrative Districts

There are 10 districts and eight counties under the jurisdiction of the Beijing Municipality.

These are four urban districts of Dongcheng, Xicheng, Chongwen and Xuanwu; four suburban districts of Chaoyang, Haidian, Fengtai and Shijingshan; two outlying suburban districts of Mentougou and Fangshan; and eight suburban counties of Changping, Shunyi, Tongxian, Daxing, Pinggu, Huairou, Miyun and Yanqing. These counties used to be the farming areas providing the urban population with vegetable and fruit supplies. But recent years have seen a rapid growth of village and township enterprises which produce a great variety of commodities not only for the domestic market but for export as well.

Culture & Education

Beijing is also the capital of China's foreign contacts. Here you will find over 150 embassies and missions, about 1,000 headquarters of foreign business corporations, import-export authorities and media people from more than 100 countries. With its new communication network and facilities, a strong scentific and technical force, well-developed industries and great market potential, Beijing attracts an ever increasing volume of foreign investment.

Language

The local dialect is what was called Mandarin Chinese in the West on which Putonghua (Standard Chinese, or, the national language) is based. Putonghua is now the common spoken language in China, while Beijingers would often add some Beijing slangs to it and putting an "er" to the last syllable of many nouns which make them sound quite strange to foreign ears.

Today foreign visitors in Beijing would often encounter young people on the street who can speak English. You would also find more and more public signs written both in Chinese and English.

Foreign Relations

Beijing has friendly ties with 96 cities in 72 countries, among which 20 cities have established relations of sister city with Beijing.

Beijing has set up 173 representative offices in foreign lands. Within the capital city, there are 134 foreign embassies, 17 representative offices of international organizations, 134 foreign mass media agencies, and about 4, 000 representative offices of overseas enterprises. There are more than 10, 000 enterprises with whole or partial foreign investment.

FAST FACTS

Visa

Foreign visitors can obtain visas from Chinese embassies and consulates with valid passports usually within a day or two. However, it is more convenient for tourists to get group visas for their China tour through Chinese travel agencies. For individual travelers, single entry visa is valid for a period within three months.

Taiwan compatriots can obtain visas from Hong Kong Office of the China Travel Service and the Hong Kong Consulate of China's Ministry of Foreign Affairs. Those who come back to the mainland via the United States, Japan and other countries can obtain travel visas from Chinese embassies and consulates in those countries.

Hong Kong and Macao compatriots should hold Reentry Cards of Hong Kong and Macao Compatriots for travel or family visits to their ancestral land.

The overseas Chinese can enter China without visas. They can enter and exit China with valid passports or other ID issued by relevant departments of the Chinese government.

Visitors should be sure to carry their passports while in China as they are needed to check into hotels, book air or train tickets, change money or establish the holder's identity.

Loss of a passport should be immediately reported to the holder's embassy or consulate, and the Foreigners Section of the Beijing Public Security Bureau. The telephone is 5255486.

Beijing and 12 other Chinese cities are authorized to issue "visas at entry port" for the convenience of increasing overseas travelers.

Visa Office of the Ministry of Foreign Affairs of the PRC
5thF Low Block, China Resources Building
26 Harbour Rd. , Wanchai

China Travel Services (HK) Ltd. (CTS)
4F CTS House
78-83 Connaught Rd. Central

China International Travel Service (HK) Ltd. (CITS)

6F South Seas Centre II
75 Mody Rd. , Tsimshatsui , Kowloon

Traveler Services
Rm. 704, Metropole Building
57 Peking Rd. , Tsimshatsui , Kowloon

Phoenix Services
Rm. B, 6F Milton Mansion
96 Nathan Rd. , Tsimshatsui , Kowloon

On Arrival

Usually three kinds of forms are distributed to passengers on board, namely Health Declaration, Entry Card and Customs Declaration. At the Beijing airport, the first counter incoming passengers come across is the Health Check-Point. Hand in your Health Declaration here. Unless you are coming from an infected area, inoculations against cholera, smallpox, typhiod and yellow fever are not compulsory. A negative AIDS test result is not required except for those planning to stay for over six months. Do not take your pets, plants or fruits as this will involve rather complicated application and sanction procedures.

The second counter is the Immigration. Passengers are required to hand in their Entry Card and passport here. If you arrive as part of a group, leave the problem to your tour operator as he is the one who brings the group visa paper.

Customs

All visitors must fill out customs declaration forms on arrival. The copy should be kept and handed in on departure. Reasonable amount of currency can be brought in, along with such personal items as alcohol and cigarettes, cameras, radios, computers and taperecorders.

Certain valuables, such as video cameras, office machines, computers and gold declared on the form must be taken out of China or else import duty will be levied on them.

Prohibited imports imclude arms, ammunition and explosives; printed matters, film or tapes detrimental to China; dangerous or narcotic drugs; and infected animals, plants or foodstuffs. It is also forbidden to take out any of these items or endangered species of animals or plants, and antiques without export permit.

Holidays & Festivals

China has 8 official celebrations and memorial days and 5 traditional festivals during the year, without taking into consideration those in minority areas.

New Year's Day	January 1, 1-day holiday
Spring Festival	The first day of the lunar calendar (usually in February) 3-day holiday
International Women's Day	March 8, 1/2-day holiday
Qingming Festival	in April
International Labor Day	May 1, 1-day holiday
Youth Day	May 4, 1/2-day holiday
Children's Day	June 1
Duanwu Festival (The Dragon Boat Festival)	5th day of 5th lunar month (usually in June)
Anniversary of the Founding of the Communist Party of China	July 1
Army Day	August 1
Zhongqiu Festival	15th day of 8th lunar month
(The Moon Festival)	(usually in September)
National Day	October 1, 2-day holiday

Chongyang Festival	9th day of 9th lunar month
(the Double Ninth	(usually in late October)
Festival)	

Spring Festival or the Chinese Lunar New Year is the most important holiday in China, comparable to that of Christmas for the Westerners. It is a time of family re-union and all members of the family head for home from all over the country several days before the festival.

Climate & Clothing

Autumn is the best season in Beijing, but lasts for a little less than two months from September to October. The average temperatures are 19.1 degrees Celsius (66.4° F) in September and 12.2° (53.9°F) in October, with an average of five rainy days. It is warm, sunny, clear and dry. A jacket will do very well, but bring along a sweater if you will stay till the end of October.

Spring is also a good time for sightseeing in Beijing. It lasts from the end of March to mid-May, with temper-atures rising from 6.5°C (43.7°F) to 18.9°C (66°F). White and purple Yulan magnolia and yellow winter jas-mine are among the earliest flowers coming into bloom. The weather is dry and windy, especially in late spring when occasionally dust storms would blow from the Gobi Desert. It is necessary to put on a warm coat. Bring sweaters with you in addition to light-weight clothes.

Summer is very hot. Temperatures from June to Au-gust average 22°C (73°F) but may reach 40°C (104°F) oc-casionally. 11 to 14 days of rain a month is expected, but rainfall is light most of the time. Dress as you would for a subtropical city, preferably in light cotton.

Winter is the longest season in Beijing, lasting for five months from November to March. In the first two months, the weather is cool and dry and the sky is pretty

blue. From the end of December to February, freezing
winds from Siberia and Mongolia cn bring the temperatures down to -10°C (15°F), but in the day-time, if it is
not windy, the temperatures are usually above 5 degrees.
Heating in hotels is turned on as early as the end of October, but most public buildings and residences have heat on
November 15 and it is turned off on March 15. Layers of
garments including thermal underwear, sweaters and
padded jackets are necessary.

The Chinese place little importance on what foreign
visitors wear so long as they are not too revealing. In
fact, some young people in Beijing are bolder than many
expected in their clothing and hair design.

Average Temperatures in Beijing

Month	Monthly Average		Average high		Average Low	
	°C	°F	°C	°F	°C	°F
Jan	-4.4	24.1	1.7	35.1	-9.7	14.5
Feb	-2.1	28.2	3.8	38.8	-7.2	19.0
Mar	4.7	40.5	11.0	51.8	-0.9	30.4
Apr	13.0	55.4	19.4	66.9	6.5	43.7
May	18.9	66.0	25.3	77.5	17.7	63.9
Jun	23.9	74.5	29.6	85.3	17.7	63.9
Jul	30.3	78.1	32.6	86.5	21.5	70.7
Aug	24.0	75.2	28.9	84.0	19.9	67.8
Sep	19.1	66.4	25.5	77.9	12.2	53.8
ct	12.2	53.9	18.7	65.7	6.8	44.2
Nov	4.3	39.7	10.0	50.0	-0.2	31.6
Dec	-2.5	27.5	3.0	37.4	-7.0	19.4

Local Time & Business Hours

Local Time   The whole of China operates within
one time zone and Beijing Time is set for every corner of

the country. China introduced daylight saving time in 1986 but gave up in 1992 as it created numerous problems and confusion.

Beijing Time is eight hours ahead of GMT and thirteen hours ahead of EST. When at noon in Beijing, the time in cities around the world is:

12 pm Hongkong/Kuala Lumpur/Manila
1 pm Seoul/Tokyo
2 pm Sydney
4 pm Auckland
6 pm Hawaii
8 pm Los Angeles/Vancouver
10 pm Chicago/Mexico City
11 pm Lima/Montreal/New York
12 pm Buenos Aires
1 am Rio de Janeiro
4 am Lisbon/London
5 am Berlin/Paris/Warsaw
6 am Cairo/Cape Town/Istanbul
7 am Baghded/Moscow/Nairobi
9 am Bombay/Karachi
11 am Bangkok/Singapore

Business Hours   In Beijing, offices are open from Monday to Friday 8.00 am to 5.00 pm with a break for lunch from 12.00 to 1.00 pm.

Shops are open on all days of the week, including public holidays. Opening hours are from 9.00 am to 8.00 pm. Parks, zoos, public libraries and museums have similar opening hours.

Privately run restaurants and snack bars are usually open all day from 6.00 am till late into the night. Most of the state-owned restaurants, however, are open from 6. 00 to 9.00 for breakfast, 10.30 am to 2.00 pm for lunch and reopen for dinner from 5 to 8 pm. Cafes and business centers in big hotels open 24 hours.

Electricity

Most better hotels have built-in converters in bathrooms for shavers, hair dryers, etc. Otherwise, come e-quipped, because there is an amazing variety of plug types in use. Generally, the voltage is 220 volt.

Water

Potable from the tap is available in only the best hotels, so visitors should always ask to make sure. Flasks of hot and cooled boiled water in rooms are telltale signs of non-potable tap water. Bottled mineral water is widely available.

International Education

Expatriates in Beijing can now stay at ease when they choose school for their children. Be it kindergarten or junior high school, the increasing number of international schools promise education up to standards in their native lands and in a cultural environment familiar to the kids.

For more information, especially matters concerning tuition, diploma and educational system used by the school, you'd better directly contact with the person in charge of enrolment at each school.

MONEY

Rmb

RMB (Renminbi, or People's Money) is the sole legal currency in the People's Republic of China.

The unit of RMB is yuan, or kuai, divided into ten jiao or mao, which are again divided into ten fen. RMB denominations: 1, 2, 5, 10, 50, and 100 yuan; smaller 1, 2, and 5 jiao and 1, 2, 5 fen coins.

Foreign Currency

Money exchange counters of the Bank of China are set up in airports, hotels and tourist stores. The exchange rate is formulated by the State Administration of Exchange Control. As a result, the exchange rate is the same wherever you change the money. You are suggested keep the form you fill when changing money, because it is necessary to show the form when you change RMB back to foreign currencies.

There is no limit to the amount of foreign currency to be brought into China, but you had better declare on your customs declaration form if the amount exceeds the equivalent of US $ 10,000. All the money exchanges are opened seven days a week from 8:00 am to 7:00 pm. The money exchanges in hotels are opened from 7:00 am to 11:00 pm.

Credit Cards & Traveler's Cheques

In Beijing most major credit cards, including the American Express, Diner's Club, Federal Card, JCB, Master Card and Visa, are accepted at hotels and certain restaurants and stores. Also useful for regular visitors to China are cards issued by Chinese banks, including the Great Wall, Peony, and Jinsui cards.

All internationally recognized traveler's cheques, in any currency, can be cashed at branches of Bank of China and money exchanges in hotels and restaurants.

AIRLINES

Beijing is s major air hub in China, with 34 interna-

tional and regional routes and 63 domestic air routes linking the capital with the world and all major cities (excluding those in Taiwan Province) and travel destinations
around China.

Twenty-six foreign airlines have their booking offices
in Beijing.

Air Ticket Booking
The booking office is located in the China Aviation
Building at 15 Xi Chang'an Jie.

There is a special counter for visitors from Hong
Kong, Macao and Taiwan, as well as for foreign passengers.

Reservation for domestic flights, call 6013336.

Reservation for international flights, call 6016667.

Capital Airport
The Capital Airport, for both international and domestic flights, is located 27 kilometers (16.8 miles) from
the city center. Taxi fare is approximately 100 yuan from
downtown area to the airport. Shuttlebuses run every 30
minutes between the China Aviation Building and the airport. The bus fare is 12 yuan.

Most of the hotels have a desk to reconfirm tickets.

For the Capital Airport Information Desk, call
4563604.

VISITORS SHOULD RECONFIRM DEPARTURE
FLIGHTS AS SOON AS THEY ARRIVE,
OR RISK HAVING THEIR BOOKINGS CANCELED!

Chinese Airlines Offices Overseas

Addis Ababa	Baghdad
Zone 4 Kefitenna 19 Kebel	Houst 7, Street 46, Area 913

57 Houst 1272/73
Tel :650337

Alma Ata
Otpar Hotel
Gao Erji Street
Tel :330170

Belgrade
Kaincka 7B Vozdovac
Tel :605555 Ext 7833

Berlin
Rm. 4004,
Clara Zetkin St.
Tel :2291964

Fukuoka
1/F Asaco Bldg.1-11-5
Tel :4726642 4728383
FAX: 4734493

Karachi
25/C 24th Street, Block 6
Tel :435570

Jakarta
Tel :5206467
FAX: 5206474

Kuwait
Suleiman Central Hilali St.
Tel :2438567

District Al Jadiryah
Tel :7769208

Bangkok
134/1-2 Silom Road

Tel :2356510 /2355250
FAX:2365279

Bucharest
Stro Cimpina 61, Sect. 1
Tel :662180

Frankfurt
Dusseldorfer Str.4

Tel :233038 6905214

Istanbul
Cumburiyet Cad 235/1
Tel :2327111
FAX:2324487

Kuala Lumpur
Ground Floor
Wisma On-Tai 161-B

Jalan Ampang
Tel :2613166
FAX: 2617422

Khabarovsk
52, 2 Tchekhova St.
Tel :37-34-40

London
41 Grosvenor Gardens
Tel :71-6300919
FAX:0293-529525

Manila
7 Cabildo St.
Urdaneta Village
Tel :8189797

Melbourne
Suite 11, 6th Floor
422 Colins Street
Tel :6421555
FAX:AA 154585

Moscow
Leninskye Gory UL.
Druzhby 6
Tel :1431560/5782725

Paris
10 Boulevard Malesher-bes
Tel :42661658

Pyongyang
330/329 Bldg. No.3
Munsudong
Tel :380-210/380-249

Rome
Corso D'Italia 29
Tel :862249

Seattle

Los Angeles
2500 Wishire Blvd.
Tel :3842703
FAX:3846103

Osaka
1/F Uchi Honmachi
Green Bldg.
Tel :946-1702

Nagasaki
1/F, Sumitomoseimei
Bldg. 7-1 Manzaimachi
Tel :28-1510
FAX:0958-28-2539

New York
45E, 49th Street
Tel :3719898/3552222

Rangoon
67 Prome Road
Tel :21927

San Francisco
51 Grant Ave.
Tel :392-2161
FAX:(415)3926214

Surabaya
Tel :511234

Singapore

1215 4th Street
Suite 310
Tel : 343-5582
FAX: 343-5244

Sharjah
78 Al Arooba St.
Sharjah Orient Bldg.
Tel : 371029

Sydney
Level 4, 70 Pitt St.
Tel : 2327895

Tokyo
3-2-7 Akasaka Minato-ku
Tel : 5052021
FAX : 5052027

Toronto
Unit 15, 131 Bloor St.
Tel : 9683300
FAX : 9685960

01-53 Anson Centre
51 Anson Road
Tel : 2252177
FAX : 2257546

Stockholm
Kungsgatan 64, 22
Tel : 216146/246172
FAX : 2257546

Zurich
Nuscheler Strasse 35
Tel : 2111617

Vancouver
1040 West Georgia St.
Tel : 6850921
FAX : 6045982

Airlines & Ticketing Offices

The booking office of Air China and other airlines is located at 15 Xi Chang'an Jie. Ticket Office Information
Tel : 6017755

Reservations for
domestic flights
Tel : 6013336

Reservations for
international flights
Tel : 6016667

Capital Airport
Information
Tel : 4563604/4563107

Air China
Domestic : 6013336
International : 6016667

China Eastern Airlines
Town Office: 6017589
6017574
Airport Office:4562135

China Northwest Airlines
Town Office:6017589
6017574
Airport Office:4562368

China Southern Airlines
Town Office: 6016899
6016799
Airport Office:4564089

China Northern Airlines
Town Office:6024078
6017594
Airport Office:4562170

China Southwest
Airlines
Town Office:6017579
5016828
Airport Office:4562870

China General Aviation
Corp.
Town Office:6024075
6024076
Airport Office:4562233
ext 3769

Xinjiang Airlines
Town Office:6024083
Airport Office:4562803

FOREIGN AIRLINES OFFICES IN BEIJING

Aeroflot (SU)
Hotel Beijing-Toronto
Tel :5002412

Air Mongolia
Tel :5018888 ext 806

Air France (AF)
China World Trade Center
Tel :5051818
FAX: 5051435

Dragonair(KA)
China World Trade Centre
Tel :5054343
FAX: 5054347

All Nippon Airways (NH)
China World Trade Centre
Tel :5050258

Ethiopian Airlines (ET)
China World Trade Center
Tel :5050314

FAX:5051188

British Airways (BA)
SCITE Tower
Tel :5124070
FAX: 5124085

Canadian Airlines (CP)
Jianguo Hotel
Tel :5001956
FAX: 5002871

EL AL Israel Airlines
(LY)
Tel :5005566 ext 1455

Japan Airlines (JL)
Changfugong Hotel
Tel :5130822
FAX: 5139865

Korean Air (KE)
China World Trade Centre
Tel :5051047

Polish Airlines (LO)
China World Trade Centre
Tel :5050136

Malaysia Airlines (MH)
Tel :5052681

Finnair (AY)
SCITE Tower
Tel :5127180
FAX:5127182

Garuda Indonesia
Tel :5052901

Iran Air
CITIC Building
Tel :5124940

Lufthansa (LH)
SCITE Tower
Tel :5123636
FAX:5124323

Pekistan Airlines (PK)
China World Trade Centre
Tel :5051681
FAX: 5052257

SAS (SK)
SCITE Tower
Tel :5120575
FAX: 5120577

Singapore Airlines (SQ)
China World /Trade Cen-
tre
Tel :5053133

FAX: 5051178

Qantas (QF)
Beijing-Toronto Hotel
Tel: 5002481
FAX: 5002022

Swissair (SR)
SCITE Tower
Tel: 5123555
FAX: 5127481

Tarom Romanian Airlines
Ritan Lu, Dong Er Jie
Tel: 5323552

United Airlines (UA)
SCITE Tower
Tel: 5128888
FAX: 5123456

Thai International (TG)
SCITE Tower
Tel: 5123881
FAX: 5123880

EMBASSIES IN BEIJING (A PARTIAL LIST)

Argentina
11 Dong Wu Jie, Sanlitun
Tel: 5322090

Australia
155 Dongzhimenwai Dajie
Tel: 5322331-7

Austria
5 Ziushui Nanjie
Dingzhimenwai
Tel: 5322061

Belgium
6 Sanlitun Lu
Tel: 5321736

Brazil
27 Guanghua Lu
Tel: 5322881

Canada
10 Sanlitun Lu
Tel: 5323536

Denmark
1 Dong Wu Jie, Sanlitun

Finland
1-10-1 Ta Yuan Building

Tel : 5322431

France
3 Dong San Jie, Sanlitun
Tel : 5322631

India
1 Ritan Donglu
Tel : 53218556

Israel
405 China World
trade Centre
Tel : 5052970-72

Luxembourg
21 Neiwubu Jie
Tel : 556175

New Zealand
1 Dong Er Jie, Sanlitun
Tel : 5322731-33

Netherlands
1-15-2 Ta Yuan Building
Tel : 5321131-34

Poland
1 Ritan Lu
Tel : 53212355

Norway
1 Dong Yi Jie, Sanlitun
Tel : 5322261

Tel : 5321817

Germany
5 Dongzhimenwai Dajie
Tel : 5322161-65

Italy
2 Dong Er Jie, Sanlitun
Tel : 5322131-34

Japan
7 Ritan Lu,
Jianguomenwai
Tel : 5322361

Malaysia
13 Dongzhimenwai Dajie
Tel : 53225531

Mexico
55 Dong Wu Jie, Sanlitun
Tel : 5322574

Philippines
23 Xiushui Beijie
Jianguomenwai
Tel : 5321872

Portugal
2-72 Ta Yuan Building
Tel : 5323497

Pakistan
1 Dongzhimenwai Dajie
Tel : 5322504

Romania
Dong Er jie, Sanlitun
Tel : 5323315

Russian Federation
4 Dongzhimen Beizhongjie
Tel : 5322051

Spain
9 Snlitun Lu

Tel : 5323629

Sri Lanka
3 Jianhua Lu, Jianguomen-
wai
Tel : 5321861

Sweden
3 Dongzhimenwai Dajie
Tel : 5323331

Switzerland
3 Dong Wu Jie, Sanlitun
Tel : 5322736-38

Thailand
40 Guanghua Lu
Tel : 5321903

United Kingdom
11 Guanghua Lu
Tel : 5321961

United States of America
3 Xiushui Beijie
Jianguomenwai
Tel : 5323831

HOTELS IN BEIJING

★★★★★
Beijing Hotel
33 Dong Chang'anjie
Tel : 5137766

Hilton Hotel Beijing
1 Dongfanglu Dongsanhuan
Beilu
Tel : 4662288

Beijing Kempinski Hotel
50 Liangmaqiaolu
Tel : 4653388

Diaoyutai State Guest House
2 Fuchenglu, Haidian
District
Tel : 8591188

China World Hotel
1 Jianguomenwai
Tel : 5052266

Great Wall Sheraton Hotel
Donghuanbeilu
Tel : 5005566

Jing Guang New
World Hotel
Hujialou, Chaoyang
District
Tel : 5018888

Kunlun Hotel
Xinyuan Nanlu,
Chaoyang District
Tel : 5003388

New Otani Chang Fu Gong
Hotel
26 Jianguomenwai Dajie
Tel : 5125555

Holiday Inn Crowne Plaza
Beijing
48 Wangfujing Dajie
Tel : 5133388

★★★★
Guang Dong Regency Ho-
tel
2 Wangfujing
Tel : 5136666

Grand Hotel Beijing
35 Dong Chang'anjie
Tel : 5137788

Palace Hotel
8 Jinyu Hutong,
Wangfujing
Tel : 5128899

Shangri-La Hotel
Beijing
29 Zizhuyuanlu
Tel : 8412211

Swissotel (Hong Kong
Macau Center)
2 Chaoyangmen beidajie
Tel : 5012288

New Century Hotel

6 Shoutinanlu
Tel : 8492001

Capital Hotel

3 Qianmen Dongdajie
Tel : 5129988

Beijing Movenpick Hotel
Xiaotianzhu, Shunyi
Tel : 4565588

Hotel Beijing-Toronto
3 Jianguomenwai
Tel : 5002266

Fragrant Hills
Hotel
Fragrant Hills Park
Tel : 2591155

Gloria Plaza Hotel
2 Jianguomen
Nandajie
Tel : 5158855

Grace Hotel
8 Jiangtaixilu,
Chaoyang District
Tel : 4362288

Jianguo Hotel
5 Jianguomenwai Dajie
Tel : 5002233

Mandarin Hotel
21 Chegongzhuang Dajie
Tel : 8319988

Peace Hotel
3 Jinyu Hutong
Tel : 5128833

China Resources Hotel
35 Jianguolu,
Chaoyang District
Tel : 5012233

Continental Grand Hotel
8 Beichen Donglu
Tel : 4915588

Grand Tower Friendship
Hotel
3 Baishiqiaolu
Tel : 8498888

Holiday Inn. Lido
Jichanglu, Chaoyang
District
Tel : 4376688

International Hotel
9 Jianguomennei Dajie
Tel : 5126688

SAS Royal Hotel
6A Beisanhuan Donglu
Tel : 4663388

Tianlun Dynasty Hotel
50 Wangfujjing Dajie
Tel : 5138888

Traders Hotel
1 Jianguomenwai Dajie
Tel : 5052277

Xiyuan Hotel
1 Sanlihe, Haidian
Distict
Tel : 8313388

Grand View Garden Hotel
88 Nancaiyuan, Xuanwu
District
Tel : 3268899

Zhaolong Hotel
2 Gongren Tiyuguanbeilu
Tel : 5002299

CVIK Hotel
22 Jianguomenwai Dajie
Tel : 5123388

Zhongyuan Hotel
18 Gaoliangqiao Xiejie
Tel : 8318888

Landmark Towers
8 Dongsanhuan Beilu
Tel : 5016688

Yuyang Hotel
18 Xinyuanxili Zhongjie
Tel : 4669988

★★★

Beijing Exhibition Center
Hotel
135 Xizhimenwai Dajie
Tel : 8316633

Dongfang Hotel

11 Wanminglu
Tel : 3014466

Jinlang Hotel
75 Chongnei Dajie
Tel : 5132288

Dragon Spring Hotel
Shuizha Beilu, Mentougou
Tel : 9843366

Beijing Asia Jinjjiang Hotel
8 Xinzhong Xijie,
Gongti Beilu
Tel : 5007788

Friendship Hotel
3 Baishiqiaolu

Tel : 8498888

City Hotel
4 Gongti Donglu,
Chaoyang District

Grand Hotel
20 Yuming Dongli
Deshengmenwai

Tel : 5007799

Guangming Hotel
Liangmaqiao,
Chaoyang District
Tel : 4678822

Holiday Inn Downtown
98 Beilishilu
Tel : 8322288

Huilongguan Hotel
Changping, Huilongguan
Tel : 2913931

Media Center
11B Fuxinglu
Tel : 8514422

Minzu Hotel
51 Fuxingmennei
Dajie
Tel : 6014466

Novotel Beijing
88 Dengshikoudajie
Tel : 5138822

Olympic Hotel
52 Baishiqiaolu, Haidian
District
Tel : 8316688

Rainbow Hotel
11 Xijinglu

Tel : 2010033

Huabei Hotel
19 Gulouwaidajie
Tel : 2028888

Huadu Hotel
8 Xinyuan Nanlu
Tel : 5001166

Chongwenmen Hotel
Chongwenmen Xidajie
Tel : 5122211

Park Hotel(Baile Hotel)
36 Puhuaangyulu
Tel : 7612233

Tiantan Hotel
1 Tiyuguanlu, Chongwen
District
Tel : 7012277

Boly Plaza
14 Dongzhimen Nandajie
Tel : 5001188

Yulong Hotel
40 Xidiaoyutai Fuchenglu

Tel : 8415588

Yanjing Hotel
19 Fuxingmenwai Dajie

Tel : 3012266

Taiwan Hotel
5 Jinyu Hutong,
Wangfujing
Tel : 5136688

21ST Century Hotel
40 Liangmaqiao
Tel : 4663311

Xinqiao Hotel
2 Dongjiaominxiang
Tel : 5133366

Yuexiu Hotel
24 Dongdajie Xuanwumen
Tel : 3014499

Chongqing Hotel
15 Guangximen Beili,
Chaoyang District
Tel : 4228888

Beiwei Hotel
13 Xijinglu, Xuanwu
District
Tel : 3012266

Desheng Hotel
14 Beisanhuan Zhonglu
Tel : 2024477

Tel : 8536688

Yanshan Hotel
138A Haidianlu
Tel : 2563388

Yanxiang Hotel
2A Jiangtailu
Tel : 4376666

Qianmen Hotel
175 Yong'anlu
Tel : 3016688

Chongwenmen Hotel
Chongwenmen Xidajie
Tel : 4228888

Tianzhao Hotel
18 Gongtidonglu,
Chaoyang District
Tel : 5080088

Overseas Chinese Hotel
5 Beixinqiao
Santiao
Tel : 4016688

Ritan Hotel
1 Ritanlu, Chaoyang
District
Tel : 5125588

Hademen Hotel
2A Chongwenmenwai
Dajie
Tel : 7012244

Guanghua Hotel
38 Donghuan Beilu
Tel : 5018866

Fangyuan Hotel
36 Dongshi Xijie
Tel : 5256331

Xizhimen Hotel
172 Xinei Dajie,
Xicheng District
Tel : 6014455

Zhumulangma Hotel
149 Gulou Xidajie,
Xicheng District
Tel : 4018822

Haoyuan Hotel
A9 Tiantan Donglu,
Chiongwen District

Furong Hotel
Balizhuang, Chaoyang
District
Tel : 5022921

Shangyuan Hotel
40 Gaoliangqiaoxiejie
Tel : 2251166

Sanyuan Hotel
9 Dongzhimen wai Xiejie
Tel : 4678288

Dadu Hotel
21 Chegongzhuang,
Xicheng District
Tel : 8319988

Zhuyuan Hotel
24 Jiu Gulou Xiaoshiqiao,
Xicheng District
Tel : 4032229

Peony Hotel
31 Huayuandonglu,
Haidian, District
Tel : 2025544

Guoan Hotel
Dongdaqiao, Chaoyang
District
Tel : 5007700

Guotai Hotel
12 Yonganxili
Jianguomenwai
Tel : 5013366

Huiqiao Hotel
19 huixindongjie,
Chaoyang District
Tel :4214061

Yueyou Hotel
13 Sanhuannanlu,
Chaoyung District
Tel :7712266

Yinghua Hotel
17 Huixindonglu,
Chaoyang District
Tel :4229830

Qinghuayuan Hotel
45 Chengfulu, Haidian
District
Tel :2573355

Ziyu Hotel
55 Zengguanglu, Haidian
District
Tel :8411188

Changchunyuan Hotel
5 Xiyuanzaochang,
Haidian District
Tel :2561177

Cuigong Hotel
76 Zhichunlu Shuangyushu,
Haidian District
Tel :2564422

Jimen Hotel
Huangtingzi Xueyuanlu,
Haidian Disteict
Tel :2012211

Ziwei Hotel
40 Shijingshanlu
Tel :8878031

Chapter 2   TOUR IN BEIJING

GETTING ABOUT

Travel by Train

It is necessary to show your passport or ID when booking or buying tickets.

For train information, call 3633622.

Beijing has four railway stations, with rail lines running to almost all provincial capitals, excluding those of Tibet, Hainan and Taiwan, and to all the major cities. A total of 252 trains depart from and arrive in Beijing each day, transporting 280,000 passengers. Soft berths, hard berths and plain seats are sold as 1st, 2nd and 3rd travel classes. Most overnight trains have dining cars.

Train Ticket Booking

It is more convenient to ask the hotel travel service or front desk to buy you a train ticket (for a small service charge) as it can sometimes be confusing and time-consuming to buy it yourself. At the Beijing Railway Station, a special counter sells tickets to foreigners and overseas Chinese. The counter is in Room 103, inside the International Lounge. Tickets can be purchased up to one week in advance.

Foreign residents, students, specialists serving in Chinese institutions, residents from Hong Kong, Macao and Tawan, as well as overseas Chinese hosted by the China Travel Service can buy tickets at the same price as domestic passengers. International students including those from Taiwan, Hong Kong and Macao can buy tickets at half price twice a year.

Suburban Travel Train

There are trains linking Beijing with outlying scenic spots. From the Beijing Railway Station, two trains run each day to bring tourists to Chengde (the former Summer Resort of the Qing Court in Hebei Province). Another train starting from the North Beijing Railway Station stops at such scenic spots as the Qinglong Bridge, Great Wall and Kangxi Grassland. Suburban trains also run from the South Beijing Railway Station and the Fengtai Railway Station to Ten Ferries (Shidu), Guanting Reservoir and the Wild Mountain Slope (Yesanpo).

Taxis

Taxis are plentiful (50,000 in all) and are always found around hotels, major department stores, main streets and can also be hired via telephone. Luxurious taxis cost for the first four kilometers 10.4 or 12 yuan and add up 1.6 to 2.5 yuan per kilometer beyond that.

The yellow mini-van (miandi) taxis cost 10 yuan flagfall and add 1.5 yuan per km after 10 kilometers.

Receipts are provided if requested. Few taxi drivers speak English so it is advisable to have destinations written out in Chinese.

For taxi complaint, call 6012620.

Taxi Service

Beijing Taxi Corp.
Tel: 8312288

Beijing Tourism Taxi Corp.
Tel: 5158605

Capital Taxi Corp.
Tel: 5138893

Beixin Taxi Corp.
Tel: 8420546

Public Transport

Public transport provides a much cheaper way to get around Beijing. The buses and trolley buses, however, are crowded most of the time. The ticket fare is very low. For tourists the most useful are Nos. 1, 4, 37, 52 and 57 buses, which run along Chang'an Avenue, passing the China World, Jinglun and Jianguo hotels, the Friendship Store and Tian'anmen Square. The fare is 50 fen (about six US cents).

No. 103 trolley bus runs through the Inner City. Sightseers can enjoy various landmarks in Wangfujing (a commercial district), Wenjinjie (former Capital Library), the Forbidden City and the White Pagoda of the Beihai Park.

Remember to avoid taking public transport in rush hours from 6:30-8:00 am or 5:00-6:30 pm.

Double Decker

Double decker is a moving window for sightseers to look at the fast changing capital city. Main routes circle through Chang'an Avenue, Qianmen Commercial District, the Second Ring Road. Along those routes are Asian Games Village, Lufthansa Shopping City, Tian'anmen Square and many other tourist attractions.

Mini Bus

Mini bus is an economical choice between the expensive taxies and crowded buses and trolley buses. Running regular services the small vans can guarantee you a seat even in rush hours and stop wherever you require along the route. Fares vary from one to six yuan.

Subway

Subway trains are fast and convenient. There are two lines. One circles the city; the other, straight line, extends from downtown area to far western suburbs.

Straight Line runs from Xidan to Pingguoyuan. Tourists can get off at Muxudi near the White Cloud Taoist Temple (Baiyunguan), the Military Museum, or the Shijingshan Amusement Park.

Major stops on the Loop Line are the Beijing Railway Station, Qianmen (near Tian'anmen Square), Xizhimen (Beijing Zoo), Yonghegong Lamasery, Dongsi Shitiao (Workers' Stadium) and Jianguomen (Old Observatory and Friendship Store).

Fuxingmen is the transfer station of the subway. One way journey costs 2 yuan. Stations are marked in *pinyin* Roman lettering). The subway operates from 5:00 am to 11:30 pm, but tourists should avoid rush hours (7:00-9:00 am and 4:30-6:00 pm).

Bicycles

Bicycles provide a form of transport for a great many Beijingers. A new comer may be stunned by the bicycle tide at rush hours.

Bicycling lanes are set aside on all major roads. The city proper is flat for easy riding and there are repair stands on the way with air pumps and spare parts. You can just point at what does not work, then shrug you shoulders if you cannot speak even one word in Chinese. The repairman will do the job.

Bicycles can be rented from large repair shops as

well as from hotels. It can be an experience to pedal around the Inner City. It takes only one and a half hours to cycle from Tian'anmen Square to the Summer Palace.

Rental charges vary from two yuan per hour for new bikes to 25 yuan for 24 hours for average ones.

Pedicabs

Pedicabs offer an alien and refreshing experience to foreign tourists. Found around big hotels and street corners, pedicabs provide a more relaxed way to tour the city, especially its narrow, zigzagging hutongs. Most pedicab charges are reasonable (from the Beijing Hotel to Tian'anmen Square, one may do well with 60 yuan). Bargaining with pedicab drivers can add extra fun.

Useful Bus Lines

Downtown Area

Trolley Bus
102
Yongdingmen Railway Station—Hufangqiao—Xidan—Zhanlan Lu—Zoo
103
Beijing Railway Station—Dong Chang'an Jie—Art Gallery—Forbidden City—Beihai Park—Zhanlan Lu—Zoo
107
Dongzhimenwai—Jiaodaokou—Drum Tower—Beihai (Back Gate)—Xizhimennei Dajie—Zoo
108
Chongwenmen—Dong Chang'an Jie—Dongfeng Bazaar—Art Gallery—Andingmen—Temple of Earth—Olympic Sports Centre—Datun

Bus

116

Temple of Heaven (South Gate)—Yongdingmen—Tian'anmen—Wangfujing—Dongdan—Yonghegong Lamasery—Hepingli

1

Gongzhufen—Military Museum—Xidan—Zhongshan Park—Wangfujing—Beijing Railway Station—Ritan Lu—Bawangfen

4

Wujiachang—Langjiayuan

5

Deshengmen—Drum Tower—Jingshan Houjie—Beihai Park—Zhongshan Park—Qianmen

10

Beijing Railway Station—Wangfujing—Tian'anmen—Xidan—Niujie Mosque—Nancaiyuan

15

Zoo—Beijing Exh. Hall—Temple of Moon—Xidan—Liulichang—Friendship Hospital—Tianqiao Market

20

Beijing Railway Station—Wangfujing—Tian'anmen—Dashalan—Temple of Heaven—Yongdingmen Railway Station

44

Xizhimen—Xizhimen (along the Second Ring Road)

Night Bus

201

Liuliqiao Nanli—Hepingjie (north end)

202

Shilipu—Huayuancun

203

Beijing Railway Station—Yongdingmen

204

Beijing Railway Station to Beijing Railway Station (circular)
(Night bus service: 11:29 pm—4:55 am, with an interval of 20 minutes)

Suburban Area Bus
302
Agricultural Exhibition Hall—Big Bell Temple
309
Tianningsi—Erqi (stops at Marco Polo Bridge)
314
Changping County seat—Ming Tombs
318
Pingguo Yuan—Fragrant Hills (Stops at China North Shooting Range, Fragrant Hills)
332
Zoo—Summer Palace
333
Summer Palace—Fragrant Hills
339
Liuliqiao—Yungang (stops at Marco Polo Bridge)
345
Deshengmen—Changping (change 314 to Ming Tombs)
347
Zoo—Badachu, Western Hills
360
Zoo—Fragrant Hills

Bus Exchange Centers for Suburban Lines
Lianhuachi (for Tanzhesi Temple) Taipingqiao Xili
Dongzhimen (for Huairou & Miyun) Dongzhimenwai Xiejie
Beijiao (for Badaling & Yanqing) Beijiao Market

TRAVEL SERVICES

Tourist Hotline 5130828

China Travel Service
Head Office
Dongjiao Minxiang
Tel : 5129933

China Int'l Travel Service
Headquarters
103 Fuxingmennei Dajie
Tel : 6011122

CITIC Travel Inc.
CITIC Building
19 Jianguomenwai Dajie
Tel : 5005920 5002255
ext 1120

China M & R Special
Tours
7A, Beihuan Xilu
Tel : 2026611 ext 41634171

CYIS Tours Corporation
Head Office
23 Dongjiao Minxiang
Tel : 5127770

China Swan Int'l Tours
Beijing Hotel
Tel : 5137766 ext 2020

China Int'l Sports Travel
4 Tiyuguan Lu
Chongwen District
Tel : 7017364 7017514

China Civil Int'l Tourist
Corp.
Jindu Hotel
Chaoyangmenwai Dajie
Tel : 5018899

Beijing Overseas Tourism
6F, Beijing tourism Tower
28 Jianguomenwai Dajie
Tel : 5158573

China Golden Bridge
Travel Service
171 A, Di'anmen Xijie
Tel : 6015993

China Goodwill Travel
Service
1F, Building No. 2
3 Baishiqiao Lu, Haidian
Tel : 8499136 8499135

China Comfort Travel
57 Di'anmen Xidajie
Tel : 6013993 6014343

China Cultural Tours Inc.
Tiantan Hotel
1 Tiyuguan Lu
Tel : 7013887 7013862

China Merchants Int'l
Travel Co.
Unit 2, Universe Building
14 Dongzhimen Nandajie
Tel : 5062228 5001188
ext 3495

China Nationality Travel
Service
1/F, Minzu Hotel
51 Fuxingmennei Dajie
Tel : 6023301 6014466
ext 2190

China Everbright
Travel Inc.
9/F, East Building
Beijing Hotel
Tel : 5137766 ext 9022

Beijing Travel Service
13 jagongfulu
Tel : 5134103 5122441

China Int'l Travel Service
Beijing
28, Jianguomenwai Dajie
Tel : 5158562

Beijing Divine Land
Travel Service
19 Xinyuan Nanlu
Dongzhimenwai
Tel : 4081619 4081306

Beijing Great Wall
Travel
Beijing Tourism Tower
28 Jianguomenwai Dajie
Tel : 4910423 4913214

China Women Travel
Service
Head Office
103, Dongsi Nandajie
Tel : 5136211
553307

Beijing North Star Int'l
Tourist Co.
10/3 Anhuili
Chaoyang District
Tel : 4911223 4910683

Beijing Zhong Bei Travel
Service
Rm. 2315 Dong Fang Hotel
Tel : 3014466 ext 23152316

Beijing China Travel Service
14 Anyuanbeili, Chaoyang
Jianguomenwai Dajie
Tel : 5158264

Beijing Tourism College
Travel Service
1, Dongzhimenwai
Panjiapo
Tel : 5024878

Beijing Youth Travel
Service
Bldg. 3, 96 Andingmennei
Dajie
Tel : 4033521

SIGHTSEEING

For many foreigners visiting Beijing, sightseeing always ranks as the number one attraction. The city of Beijing has long been famous for its rich and fascinating collections of historical sites and scenic spots.

IMPERIAL PALACES

The Forbidden City

Officially known as the former Imperial Palace or Gu Gong, most foreigners prefer the name it was given to indicate that only the royal family and ministers, plus the occasional ambassador bearing tribute, were allowed into this small city where antique customs were preserved until the 1920s.

It was originally built by more than 200,000 men in the early 14th century for the third Ming Emperor Yongle, and rebuilt and renovated many times later, but always according to the original design.

With 9,000 bays in a total area of 74 hectares (183 acres) the city is divided into three parts. The first has four monumental gates and a stream spanned by five marble bridges. The magnificent Gate of Supreme Harmony, with its guard of bronze lions, leads to the area of flagstones designed to accommodate 9,000 people for imperial ceremonies and the Hall of Supreme Harmony, which is filled with treasures relating to those ceremonies, such as bronze incense burners and jade chimes.

Beyond are the halls of the Inner Court, which were living quarters of the court. Within this area are small courtyards and palaces that are now used as museums housing the imperial collections of paintings, calligraphy, sculptures, ancient pottery, bronzes, clocks, and everyday items.

In the rear is a garden of ancient cypress and pine trees and the well in which Empress Dowager Cixi drowned a concubine who challenged her power.

Buses: 2, 10, 20, 101

Trolley Buses: 103, 109

Temple of Heaven Park (Tiantan)

Built between 1406 and 1420, the complex of buildings that make up the Temple of Heaven covers 273 hectares and represents the greatest achievements of Ming and Qing architecture. The complex is laid out according to the needs of sacred ceremony, because it was believed to be the one place on earth with direct access to heaven, although only for the emperors who were regarded as celestial go-betweens.

The main building that has rightly become a symbol of Beijing is the Hall of Prayer for Good Harvests. The original was burnt down in 1889 but faithfully reconstructed. The hall has 28 wooden pillars supporting a 39-meter-high tower of three conical roofs, covered with blue glazed tiles, to reflect the color of the sky. The wooden walls are richly decorated, inside and out.

From the Gate of Prayer for Good Harvests to the Bridge of Vermilion Stairs, there is a raised walkway that leads to the Imperial Vault of Heaven. Today it is best known for the wall that surrounds it, called the Echo or

Whispering Wall because of its remarkable acoustics design that carries sound so well. To the south of the vault is the Circular Mound, an open-air altar consisting of three round marble terraces. This is where the emperors would offer up their prayers.

To the west of the complex is the Hall of Abstinence, where the emperors would prepare themselves for the solemn occasion by spending a night without food or wine.

Buses: 6, 15, 20, 39, 43
Trolley Buses: 106, 116
Open: 8:30-17:00

Jingshan Park

Also known as Coal Hill (Meishan), this hill, directly north of the Forbidden City, owes its popular name to the time during the Ming Dynasty when an artificial hill was made with earth from the excavated moat of the Forbidden City. A story tells that the emperor kept emergency supplies of coal hidden in the hill.

On the summit of the 43 meter mound is the Ten Thousand Springs Pavilion, which used to be the highest point in the city and which on clear days commands fabulous views of the former Imperial Palace, Beihai Lake and the Drum and Bell Towers.

Today the site is a Children's Palace, with facilities for sports, art, music and scientific activities.

Another place worth seeing is the Miaoguan Pavilion where the last Ming emperor hanged himself from a locust tree on hearing that a peasant uprising army was storming the city.

Bus: 101
Trolley Buses: 103, 109
Open: 7:00-20:00

Beihai Park

Situated in the center of Beijing, Beihai Park was an imperial garden of the Jin, Yuan, Ming and Qing dynasties, with a history of 800 years. It was built between 1166 and 1179, then named Taining Palace, or Supreme Tranquility Palace. Later in the Yuan, Ming and Qing dynasties, it was steadily expanded into a garden with a picturesque scenery of green hills and clear waters. It occupies an area of 68.2 hectares, 29.3 of which is land and the rest is water surface. The Italian traveler Marco Polo loved this "celestial garden" when he was invited by the Yuan Emperor to visit it.

The main buildings are Tuan Cheng (Round Town), Yong'an Temple (Eternal Peace Temple), Nine-Dragon Screen (one of China's three remaining such screens), and Paradise Hall.

The center of the park is Qionghua Islet, or Gem Islet, with a white pagoda on top. The islet is heavily forested, with pavilions, platforms and houses delicately designed.

Bus: 101

Trolley Buses: 103, 107, 109, 111

Zhongshan Park

Built in 1421, it was the sacrificial altar of the Ming and Qing courts. In front of the park is Tian'anmen Square. To the south is the Golden Water River. Beyond the moat on the northern side is the Forbidden City. The Sacrificial Altar and attached buildings, generally called the Inner Altar, dominate the center of the park. The surrounding halls and palaces are named the Outer Altar.

It was a place where the emperors offered sacrifices to the God of Earth and the five gods of different cereals. The rectangular altar is the symbol of the earth. According to Chinese ancient philosophy, the altar is divided into five parts, filling with black, red, white, green and yellow earth. It symbolized that all parts of the world under heaven belonged to the Emperor, the Son of Heaven. Built in the early 15th century, the wooden Prayer Hall north of the altar was the rest room for the emperor before he attended the sacrificial ceremony.

In 1925, the coffin of Dr. Sun Yat-sen was laid here, thus the hall was renamed the Zhongshan Hall in 1928 in memory of the great revolutionary.

Buses: 1, 4, 10, 20O
pen: 7:00-20:00

The Working People's Cultural Palace

The site, located east of the Gate of the Heavenly Peace, was the Imperial Ancestral Temple where the emperors of the Ming and Qing dynasties paid tribute to their forefathers.

Built in 1544, the emperor offered sacrifices to ancestors here on grand occasions, such as coronation, imperial wedding, appointment of regency and the triumphant return of an expedition army.

Three grand halls dominate the palatial complex. Further to the south is the Jade Belt River, on which there are five exquisite marble bridges.

Buses: 1, 4, 10, 20O
pen: 8:00-20:00

Drum and Bell Towers

In old times all Chinese cities had drum and bell towers to sound the time of day and announce curfew. In Beijing the two are found in a direct meridian line north of the Forbidden City. The Drum Tower (Gulou) was first built in 1272, but reconstructed in 1420 when the Ming Dynasty established its capital in Beijing. It rises from a brick podium with a tower pierced by six gates and topped by a roof of upturned eaves.

To the north is the Bell Tower (Zhonglou), first constructed in 1420 and rebuilt in 1747 during the reign of Emperor Qianlong. The original iron bell was replaced by a giant bronze bell, which was rung at seven o'clock every evening until 1924.

Bus: 8
Trolley Bus: 107
Open: 8:30-16:00

Summer Palace (Yiheyuan)

Situated 20 kilometers northwest of downtown Beijing, the Summer Palace was used by the court as a resort from the capital's heat for 800 years. During the Qing Dynasty it became a fashionable royal resort and venue of extravagant celebrations. Empress Dowager Cixi made it her summer residence and spent vast amounts of money (much from the state treasury) to create a veritable paradise.

It was badly damaged by the Anglo-French troops during the Second Opium War of 1860 and further devastated in 1900 by the Allied Forces of Eight Foreign Powers following the Boxer Rebellion. Since then much has been restored and the palace with its immense, classic Kunming Lake, is a favorite summer retreat for Beijingers.

The lake covers three quarters of the total 1,290 hectares and contains small islands, ornamental bridges and the famous Marble Boat, which was once a teahouse. On shore, at the foot of Longevity Hill (Wanshoushan), are the former imperial residences, filled with Cixi's furniture and personal belongings. One building contains a theater museum that recalls the Empress Dowager's passion for theatricals, and in the garage is the first automobile imported into China, a Mercedes Benz. Among other attractions are the Long Corridor on the lake shore, the bronze pavilion weighing 444,000 kg, the court-cuisine restaurant in the Pavilion for Listening to the Orioles, and the newly-restored Suzhou Street, with shops selling items that once entertained the court.

Buses: 332, 374, 375

Open: 8:00-16:00

Fragrant Hills (Xiangshan)

Situated 28 kilometers northwest of downtown Beijing, this park had long been a favorite summer retreat of the emperors. In the 12th century it was a royal hunting park. Its focal point is the Incense Burner Peak (Xianglufeng)—557 meters above sea level. On top is a huge rock that resembles an incense burner. A temple was built in the hills before 1186 and in 1745 the Garden of Tranquility and Pleasure (Jingyiyuan) was built.

It is a popular place in autumn when the smoke tree leaves turn red, and many scholars have eulogized the park. It is also famous for its snow scenery in winter.

Buses: 360, 333

Open: 8:30-16:00

The Ruins of Yuanmingyuan

Yuanmingyuan was the most glorious imperial garden ever built through the Chinese history, known as "garden of gardens". The huge area on northwestern outskirt was actually divided into three individual gardens: Yuanmingyuan (Garden of Perfection and Brightness), Wanchunyuan (Garden of Ten Thousand Springs) and Changchunyuan (Garden of Ever-lasting Spring), centered around Fuhai (Lake of Happiness). Its construction started in 1709 and took 150 years to complete. The Qing Dynasty assembled the best building materials and employed armies of skillful craftsmen nationwide to design and build 40 scenic spots and 145 large buildings, in which many contained invaluable artifacts and treasures. All scenic spots were interconnected by long corridors, walls and bridges.

Unfortunately, the Anglo-French joint forces in 1860 looted all treasures in the garden and burned it to ashes. In 1900, the Allied Forces of Eight Foreign Powers invaded Beijing and sacked the remaining buildings. The ruins of the garden are well preserved for visitors to ponder on the past.

Bus: 364

Open: 8:30-16:00

Tian'anmen Square

The square, located in the heart of modern Beijing, covers 44 hectares. The largest square in the world can accommodate 500,000 people. The founding ceremony of the People's Republic of China was held here on October 1, 1949, which climaxed with 1 million people gathering to hear the late Chairmen Mao Zedong proclaim the birth of New China.

The Gate of Heavenly Peace (Tian'anmen), 33.7 meters in height, is an imposing symbol of the city, Its huge tower (now open to visitors) is crowned by a double-eaved, glazed tile roof. Over its central arched gateway is a portrait of Mao Zedong, to the east is the Working People's Cultural Palace and to the west is Zhongshan Park, dedicated to Dr. Sun Yat-sen. On the eastern side of the square is the Museum of Chinese History and the Museum of the Chinese Revolution. One the western side of the square is the Great Hall of the People, built in 1959 to house the National People's Congress, China's parliament. In the middle of the square is the Monument to the People's Heroes and Chairman Mao's Memorial Hall, where the former leader lies enshrined in a crystal coffin.

A grand flag-hoisting ceremony is held every morning. Accompanied by music played by a military band, the guard of honor of the three service in full dress hoists China's national flag at sunrise. The ceremony has become a new attraction for sightseers and pedestrians.

Buses: 1, 4, 10, 57

Great Wall (at Badaling and Mutianyu)

One of the world greatest tourist attractions, the Great Wall was built section-by-section between the fifth century B.C. and the 16th century A.D. It was called the Wall of Ten Thousand Li which translates as 5,000 kilometers or 3,333 miles, and was designed to keep out nomadic invaders from the north.

The statistics are as awesome as the wall. One section reportedly took 300,000 men to build in 10 years. Stretching between regular watchtowers, the wall winds from the Bohai Gulf to the Jiayuguan Pass in Gansu Province. Much is now in ruins, but several sections have been restored. The best known is at Badaling, 80 kilometers (50 miles) north of downtown Beijing. Here visitors can climb or take a cable car to the top of the wall. This section, built during the Ming Dynasty, is 7.8 meters high and 5.8 meters wide.

Another superbly restored section of the wall is at Mutianyu, a few miles to the east from Badaling. It can be reached by long flights of steps or a cable car from the foot of the mountain.

A Chinese saying goes: "One's life is not completed if he has not climbed the Great Wall".

Tourist Buses: Depart daily from Qianmen, Chongwenmen, Dongdaqiao and Zhanlanlu

Open: 8:30-16:00

Taoranting Park

The park with charming natural landscape was once one of the royal brick kilns for the construction of the new capital in the Ming Dynasty.

Today the park is heavily forested with carefully laid out lakes and islets. Pavilions of various styles create a new summer retreat in the city for Beijingers, especially for Peking Opera fans.

Buses: 5, 14

Trolley Bus: 102

Open: 7:00-20:00

Ming Tombs

Some 50 kilometers northwest of downtown Beijing. A tour to the Ming Tombs is generally combined with a visit to the Great Wall. The 13 tombs of the Ming emperors are spread around a valley that looks like a natural courtyard with an entrance guarded by huge stone animals. Of the tombs only the underground burial chambers of Dingling, the mausoleum of Ming Emperor Wanli who reigned from 1573 to 1620, are open to the public after being excavated in 1956. On display in the museum are marble conffins, religious regalia, jewelry, garments, procelain and curios.

Tourist Buses: Depart daily from Qianmen, Chongwenmen, Dongdaqiao and Zhanlanlu

Open: 8:30-17:00

Badachu (Eight Great Sites)

Badachu Park, featuring eight ancient temples in Beijing's Western Hills, covers an area of 3,000 hectares. The eight shrines and temples were built from the Sui Dynasty in the sixth century till the Qing Dynasty in the last century. Lingguang Temple established its reputation for the storage of a Buddha's tooth. Thousands of apricot trees in the hills are in full blossom in April. A 1,050-meter-long cable with 100 double-seat chairlifts offers a bird's-eye-view at tourists' uphill journey.

An adventurous activity is to slide down from the summit at a maximum speed of 80 km per hour along a 1,700-meter-long rollertrail with more than 50 curves.

Buses: 347, 311, 389
Open: 8:30-17:00

Beijing Zoo

The zoo, China's largest, has a great collection of rare animals especially the giant panda. Altogether there are some 5,000 animals of over 570 species in the zoo. It used to be a private garden of a Qing aristocrat. The zoo was first established by Empress Dowager Cixi. She imported 700 creatures from Germany for entertainment. Many of the animals come from different parts of China and abroad, including giant sea-turtle, tiger, little panda and Tibetan yak.

Buses: 7, 15, 19, 45, 27
Trolley Buses: 103, 107, 111
Open: 8:30-16:00

Grand View Garden (Daguanyuan)

This park in the southwest corner of the city is one of Beijing's newest attractions. It was created in 1986 and modeled on the garden described in the Chinese classic novel *A Dream of Red Mansions* by Cao Xueqin. it contains a carefully landcaped lake, surrounded by stylized stones, forests and rockery hillocks, and pavilions constructed of wood and bricks according to Qing tradition. The buildings are named after those in the book, such as "Bamboo Lodge", "Studio of Autumn Freshness", "Lotus Fragrance Pavilion", "Warm Scented Arbor" and so on.

Bus: 61

Open: 8:30-16:30

Beijing Botanical Garden

Located at the foot of the Fragrant Hills, the botanical garden occupies an area of 100 hectare. Inside the garden there are 130,000 woody plants and 116 varieties of herbs. The ground is subdivided into a dozen of small flower gardens, such as peony, lilac, and lily. Adjacent to the garden there are several scenic spots, including the Temple of Sleeping Buddha, Valley of Cherry and Memorial Hall of Cao Xueqin.

Buses: 333, 360
Open: 8:30-16:00

Marco Polo Bridge (Lugouqiao)

The popular name for the bridge is derived from the Venetian traveler's description in his famous *Travels*. It also gained fame for its unique workmanship.

The bridge was built in the early 12th century, over the Yongding River to cover the access to the capital, 16 kilometers west of downtown Beijing. Stretching 266.5 meters and supported by 11 arches, it is most famous for the parapets on either side, with 140 columns with lion sculptures on top. Local people say the lions are so many one cannot find how many they really are.

Two stone tablets at each end record the rebuilding of the bridge. It is one of the eight grand sights in old Beijing.

The bridge is where the war to resist Japanese aggression began at the outset of World War II in 1937.

Bus: Change 309 from Tianningsi

China Ethnic Culture Garden

China is home to 56 ethnic groups, each with a diverse cultural heritage, different customs and costumes, and unique arts and crafts. Located adjacent to the National Olympic Sport Center, the garden features replicas of buildings in ethnic regions and song and dances played by performers of the local people.

Buses: 380 or No. 2 double decker
Open: 8:30-17:30

The World Park

On an area of 46.7 hectares the largest theme park in China has mini-replicas of 106 renowned scenic spots from 30 countries, including the Great Pyramid, the Effiel Tower and the White House.

A tourist bus departs from Xibianmen
Open: 8:00-18:00

Old Beijing Mini Landscape Park

Located in Nankou Town, 40 kilometers northeast of downtown Beijing, the park is a reconstruction of the old Beijing in its prime time in miniature. It features more than 100 carefully carved buildings with tiny bricks and tiles, revealing the flourishing capital of the Qing Empire. Many scenes are no more than names on maps of present-day Beijing.

Bus: 345 from Deshengmen
Open: 9:00-17:00
Mini-bus from Beijing Zoo

Beijing Shisanling Waxwork Palace of Ming Dynasty

A new theme park built near the Ming Tombs next to Old Beijing Mini Landscape Park, the palace presents historical scenes with exquisite wax figures, depicting events happened centuries ago.

Tourist Buses: Depart daily from Qianmen, Chongwenmen, Dongdaqiao and Zhanlanlu
Open: 8:30-17:00

MUSEUMS

Most museums open from 9:00 am till 4:00 pm, and close on Mondays.

Museum of Chinese History
Built in 1959 on the east side of Tian'anmen Square, it is China's largest state museum in which more than 60, 000 antiques, historic documents and pictures are stored. It is a historic tunnel to review the evolution of the Chinese nation.

Museum of the Chinese Revolution
Formally opened in 1961, the museum keeps some 120,000 pieces of relics, pictures and documents on Chinese revolution since the May 4 Movement in 1919, especially those after the founding of the Chinese Communist Party in 1921.

Military Museum of the Chinese People's Revolution
An architecture built to celebrate the 10th anniversary of New China, the museum now displays weapons and equipment for military use. The exhibits convey the evolution of weapons from pre-historic shield and sword to rocket in the nuke era.

Capital Museum
Located in the tranquil Temple of Confucius, the museum keeps some 80, 000 pieces of antiques of the Yuan, Ming and Qing dynasties. An annual temple fair is held at the Spring Festival, portraying the ceremonial ritual in memory of Confucius.

Beijing Museum of Natural History
Located on Yongdingmen Street in Chongwen Dis-

trict, the museum highly summarizes the development of living beings in the last 300-400 million years. Changes of the universe and a mini-Jurassic Park are shown here.

Geological Museum

Situated on Yangrou Hutong in Xicheng District, the museum is composed of six exhibition halls featuring mineral resources, the history of the earth, Paleozoic plants and animals, mineral deposits, gems and jade.

China Physical Culture Museum

Built for the 11th Asian Games, it is the only museum featuring physical culture. The four halls display Chinese ancient sports, contemporary sports, sports achievements of New China and Chinese ethnic sports.

China Art Gallery

The museum boasts of a rich collection of masterpieces by famous Chinese painters and sculptors. Located on Wusi Street, Dongcheng District, it is also the most important venue for art exhibitions in the capital city. Some 100 Chinese and foreign exhibitions are held here every year.

Aviation Museum

The largest aviation museum in Asia has 140 aircraft of different times, including planes for China's late top leaders. Visitors can also take a China-made Yun-5 plane for an air tour. Beijing Planetarium The planetarium on Xizhimenwai Dajie has a planetarium hall, a lecture hall, an exhibition hall and an observatory. The planetarium hall shows the movements of the sun, the moon and other stars.

China Arts and Crafts Gallery

It is a large art gallery for storage, exhibition, collection and sales of Chinese art and craft items. The treasure trove on the fifth floor keeps 500 pieces of craft masterpieces. The gallery is located in the same building of Parkson Shopping Center.

Yan Huang Art Gallery

Run by Huang Zhou, a renowned Chinese painter, the gallery collects paintings by ancient masters. It also offers a venue for artists and amateurs to exchange news and views about Chinese art. It is located inside the National Olympic Center.

Museum of the Dabaotai Tombs of the Western Han Dynasty

The museum, located atop a tomb of Western Han Dynasty at Guogongzhuang Village of Fengtai District, is composed of a mausoleum and exhibition rooms with excavated funeral objects of the Han emperors and their wives.

Site of Peking Man (Zhoukoudian)

Several decades ago, local farmers minding limestone in Zhoukoudian, 48 kilometers (30 miles) southwest of downtown Beijing, came upon some bone fossils and called them "the Dragon Bones". Zhoukoudian became known as "Dragon Bone Mountain". Drugstores purchased the bones as a medical ingredient. The news about the "magic bones" drew attention of scientists.

In 1929 these limestone caves became world famous with the discovery of a skull and two teeth dating back 200,000 to 500,000 years. They were named "Homo erectus pekinensis", or Peking Man. But the fossils were lost during World War II. Many of the implements used by those early humans, and bones of animals they hunted are on display at a museum near the site of the discovery.

The Imperial Archives (Huangshicheng)

Situated at the southern end of Nanchizi Street, the Imperial Archives keeps the complete profiles of the royal families of the Ming and Qing courts.

With a history of 450 years, the complex is composed of the grand gate, the main hall and attached palaces. It preserves a large number of royal archives, including the imperial edicts (Holy Instructions), some volumes of the *Great Encyclopedia of Yongle* and the *Complete Collection of Books of the Qing Dynasty*. A treasure of the archives are the family profiles of the Qing royal family. The huge documents, 80 centimeters long, 45 centimeters wide and 1 meter thick in a bound volume, weigh about 150 kilograms, known as the "king of books".

Stone Sculpture Art Museum

Located in the Temple of Five Pagodas, the museum has 6,000 stone sculptures of different dynasties.

MEMORIAL HALLS

Memorial Hall of Chinese People's War of Resistance Against Japanese Aggression

The hall is located in Wanping Town near the Marco Polo Bridge where the eight-year-long anti-Japanese War broke out in 1937. A huge wall-size oil painting with video and sound effects depicts the historic war.

Memorial Hall of Chairman Mao Zedong

The hall, completed in August, 1977, is in memory of the late Chairman Mao. The crystal coffin of the Chairman is placed in the center of the hall for visitors to

pay their homage. Also displayed are antiques of other
Chinese leaders: Zhou Enlai, Liu Shaoqi and Zhu De.

Memorial Hall of Lu Xun

It is located on Fuchengmennei Dajie near the Temple of White Pagoda in the east and a courtyard where Lu
Xun lived in the 1920s. Lu, one of China's greatest contemporary writers and thinkers, wrote many of his essays
and novels in the small courtyard garden. The hall has an
exhibition about Lu Xun's life.

Memorial Hall of Xu Beihong

Exhibits include Chinese-style and Western oil paintings, created by Xu at different times. Also displayed are
photos and objects used by the painter in his life.

Memorial Hall of Mei Lanfang

Mei, the greatest Peking Opera Master, created
many famous female roles and helped bring about a gold-
en age of Peking Opera in the 1920s. His residence where
he spent his last decade opens to the public to show the
life and achievements of the late actor.

Memorial Hall of Cao Xueqin

Nestled in a valley of the Fragrant Hills, it is believed to be the birthplace of A *Dream of Red Mansions,*
one of China's greatest literary classics. Inside the hall are
the living quarter and study of Cao Xueqin, the author of
the novel.

Memorial Hall of Soong Ching Ling

Once the mansion of a Qing prince regent (father of
China's last emperor), the delicate garden had been the
living quarter of Soong Ching Ling—widow of Dr. Sun
Yat-sen—since she moved from Shanghai in 1963 till her

death in 1981. Her life is an epitome of Chinese contemporary history.

Memorial Hall of Shen Yanbing

The great writer spent his last six years in the residence. Now there is an exhibition to display his manuscripts, photos and other documents.

Double-Spring Villa

It is an exquisite garden in the Fragrant Hills on the western outskirts of Beijing. In 1949, the Central Committee of CPC and China's top leaders chose the villa as their temporary residence before moving to Zhongnanhai in the city. Now an exhibition shows what happened at the time.

NATURAL LANDSCAPES

Those who are fed up with the maddening metropolis can find pure natural scenery in suburban Beijing. As the highways extend to all directions and more holiday resorts are being built, the faraway mountains are now reachable for weekend excursions.

Shangfang Mountain

Shangfang Mountain, located in Fangshan District, is more than 70 kilometers southwest of downtown Beijing. Famous for its picturesque scenery, the mountain consists of nine caves and 12 peaks. Legend has it that Monk Huayan built temples and pagodas on Shangfang Mountain as early as over 1,900 years ago in the Eartern Han Dynasty.

An expressway leads directly to the foot of the mountain. Tourists may climb up the mountain either by way of the Nunnery of Great Mercy or via the 262-step Heavenly Ladder dug out of the mountainside 500 years ago. In the eastern part of the mountain, visitors will find several nunneries and a 29-meter-high pine tree.

Built in the early Tang Dynasty, the Temple of shangfang used to be the center of the 72 nunneries. Its main hall still retains the architectural style of the Ming Dynasty. Three Ming stone tablets in the courtyard record the rises and falls of the monastery.

Take train at Yongdingmen Railway Station and get off at Gushankou Station.

Yunshui Cave

Located 70 kilometers southwest of downtown Beijing, the 620-meter-long Yunshui Cave is one of the largest calcareous karst caves in northen China. There are six naturally formed halls inside, with an average height of 6 meters. The cave is full of various lifelike stalactites, among which the tallest is 37 meters high.

Take train at Yongdingmen Railway Station and get off at Gushankou.

Cave of Stone Flowers

Located 100 kilometers southwest of downtown Beijing, the cave has six floors which are closely linked with each other. Two floors, measuring 1,222 meters in total length, are open to the public. Vertical distance between these two floors is over 40 meters, equivalent to the height of a 14-story building.

The cave has many stalactites in shapes of monkeys, lions, peacocks, etc. A cauliflower-shaped crystal-clear stalactite is the first of its kind ever found in a cave in China.

Change a long distance bus at Fangshan Station to the cave.

Open: 9:00-16:00

Shidu (Ten Ferries)

Ninety kilometers southwest of downtown Beijing, the Juma River, originating from the Taihang Mountains in Shanxi Province and flowing 46 kilometers before joining the sea in Hebei Province, zigzags ten times in the mountains in Fangshan District, forming ten ferries. Hence the name Shidu.

With beautiful mountain peaks reflected in water, this area can match the beauty of the Li River landscape in Guilin. A gigantic rock of about 10 meters high named Terrace of Viewing Buddha stands by the ninth ferry. Looking from a small pavilion built on the rock, the rock resembles a stone Buddha.

Take a bus at Lianhuachi Long Distance Bus Station, or take train at Yongdingmen Railway Station at 6:08 or 6:58 am.

Hudongshui Scenic Area

The scenic area is situated in a 10-kilometer-long canyon, 100 kilometers northeast of downtown Beijing. The scenic area runs six kilometers from east to west and 1.5 kilometers from north to south. Hudongshui literally means lake, cave and water which tourists can easily find here. The place is abundant in mulberries, apricots and peonies. And the congenial climate in the heavily-forested Hudongshui attracts birds to build their nests.

East Beijing Canyon in Pinggu County stretches some six kilometers in length with steep cliffs and spectacular waterfalls.

Take a bus at Dongzhimen and change another bus at Pinggu.

White Dragon Pool

Located 25 kilometers northeast of Miyun County seat, it is known for its three waterfalls that are chained one to anther. The pool is situated between two mountains where many kinds of trees including pine and fruit trees are abundant. This mountainous area is teemed with strangely-formed rocks. To the west of the pool lies the Miyun Reservoir.

Since the Song and Yuan dynasties, a large number of temples and temporary imperial palaces were built here, including the Temple of Five Dragons.

Some tourist facilities have been built to the north of the pool, including a holday village, a castle-like hotel, a swimming pool and a small hunting field.

Take a bus at Dongzhimen Long-distance Bus Station.

Jinhai Lake

Ninety kilometers northeast of downtown Beijing in Pinggu County, Jinhaihu Park boasts beautiful mountains and a vast lake. It offers a wide range of recreational programs including boating, parachuting over the water, fishing and swimming.

Take a bus at Dongzhimen Long-Distance Bus Station.

Miyun Reservoir

The largest reservoir in North China covers an area of 188 square kilometers and can store 4.375 billion cubic meters of water. it is one of the major water supply reservoirs for Beijing. A 110-km-long highway circles the reservoir. The temperature is three centigrade lower than that in the urban area, offering an ideal summer retreat.

Take a bus from Dongzhimen Long-distance Bus Station.

Kangxi Grassland

The Kangxi Grassland of 32,000 acres lies next to Guanting Lake on the west and the Haituo Mountain on the north. It boasts a landscape of mountain peaks, water trees and grassland. Temperatures here average 8.4 °C lower than in the famous summer resorts in Chengde and Beidaihe. A lot of amusement and tourist facilities have been built, including a folklore holiday village, a race course, an outdoor sport field, and a labyrinth.

Take train at Xizhimen Railway Station and get off at Kangzhuang.

Yunxiugu Scenic Area

The gorge in Miyun County is three kilometers long. Three giant rocks are remains of a glacier of the Quaternary Period. Also inside the gorge is a large kiwi fruit orchard.

Take a bus from Dongzhimen Long-Distance Bus Station.

Songshan Natural Reserve

The national natural reserve is located in Yanqing County, 90 kilometers north of downtown Beijing. The scenic area is known for the hot springs. Rising 2,199 meters above sea level, Songshan Mountain is Beijing's second highest mountain. The reserve is home to more than 180 species of animals and 700 types of plants.

Take a bus from Dongzhimen Long-Distance Bus Station.

Yanqi Lake

Located in Huairou County, 100 kilometers north of downtown Beijing, Yanqi Lake is a waterborne amusement park. Activities on the lake include dragon-boat rid-

ing, yachting and parachute surfing. When the day is
warm, people can go swimming or get sun-tanned on an
artificial beach. Other interesting scenic spots in Huairou
are the Mutianyu Section of the Great Wall, the Shen-
tangyu (literally meaning God's Canyon), the Buddhist
Hongluo Temple, the quiet Miyun Reservoir and the
primitive Yunmeng Mountains.

Take a bus from Dongzhimen Long-Distance Bus
Station.

Longqing Gorge

Longqing Gorge, an "Old City with Nine Windings"
as the ancients called it, is a natural gorge located 10 kilometers from Yanqing County seat. A deep, quiet and tor-
tuous reservoir stretches over 7 kilometers inside the
gorge.

Tourists can enjoy its varied scenery—as exquisite as
that in South China and as vigorous as that in North China. With its exquisite natural scenery and delightful
weather, Longqing Gorge has become one of Beijing's
tourist attractions.

Scheduled bus departs at Beijiao Maket Long-Distance Bus Station.

WORSHIP PLACES

Yonghegong Lamasery

This lamasery, also known as the Palace of Harmony
and Peace, was built as the residence of Emperor
Yongzheng of the Qing Dynasty in his princehood. When
the young prince ascended the throne, the mansion was
converted to a temple according to traditions.

During the reign of Emperor Qianlong, it became a
center of learning for the Yellow Hat Sect of Tibetan

Lamaism, and at certain period housed a community of 1,
500 Tibetan, Mongolian and Han lamas, as well as a Living Buddha. Today there are about 70 Mongolian lamas in
residence.

The temple consists of five halls, connected by five
courtyards and three archways with exquisitely carved
eaves. The prayer halls contain many superb statues—including the 23-meter-high Maitreya, carved with a single
white sandalwood tree brought from Tibet, as well as Tibetan scriptures and a great copper cauldron. The Great
Stele Pavilion has a square stone inscribed with Lamaist
scriptures in Chinese, Manchu, Mongolian and Tibetan.

Buses: 13, 116
Subway: No. 1
Open: 8:30-16:00

Big Bell Temple (Dazhongsi)

Located on the North Third Ring Road (Beisan-
huanlu), this small temple was built in 1733 and named
Juxingsi, or the Temple of Awakening. Ten years later a
huge bell was installed in it, and the name was changed.
The bell was cast in the reign of Ming Emperor Yongle
and has a diameter of 3.3 meters. It is almost seven meters (nearly 23 feet) high and weighs 46.5 tons. It is inscribed with the texts of 17 Buddhist scriptures, a total of
227,000 Chinese characters, that are believed to be the
work of Shen Du, a renowned Ming calligrapher. The
bell gives off a deep, sonorous sound which can be heard
over 10 kilometers away.

The temple also houses about 100 other bronze bells
from the Yuan, Ming and Qing dynasties, all showing
distinctive patterns and a very high degree of workmanship.

Buses: 302, 367
Open: 8:30-17:30

Sleeping Buddha Temple (Wofosi)

Located on the eastern side of the Fragrant Hills, this temple was built in the seventh century at the heyday of the Tang Dynasty. It was enlarged in the Yuan Dynasty to accommodate a huge bronze reclining Buddha, which was cast in 1320 using 25,000 kilograms of bronze.

The Sleeping Buddha, 5.2 meters long, is said to portray the nirvana of Sakyamuni, founder of Buddhism. Surrounding the Buddha are 12 smaller sculptures, depicting the mourning expression of his 12 disciples. Also contained in the temple are Buddhist scriptures and other statues.

Buses: 360, 333
Open: 8:30-17:00

Temple of Azure Clouds (Biyunsi)

Generally considered the most magnificent of all the temples in the Western Hills, the temple was built during the Yuan Dynasty and established its reputation during the Ming Dynasty. It was a favorite retreat for emperors and their wives. It was expanded in Emperor Qianlong's reign. Early this century, the temple was the original burial place of Dr. Sun Yat-sen. A memorial tomb still remains in the temple after the coffin was removed to Nanjing.

The temple is built on six different levels, and each of the interconnecting courtyards has a special character. The Hall of Five Hundred Arhats is modeled on Jingci Temple in Hangzhou. The figures, 1.5-meter-high, with their unique expressions stand in rows in the building.

Bus: 360, 333
Open: 8:30-17:30

Tanzhe Temple (Tanzhesi)

A local saying goes that "the history of Tanzhe Temple is longer than that of Beijing City. " This temple dates back 1,600 years when it was called Jiafusi, or the Temple Auspicious Fortune. During the Tang Dynasty it was renamed Longquansi, or Temple of Dragon Spring, because of the pool in the rear. It later assumed its present name, which means Pool and Wild Mulberry.

The temple is built on a hillside and consists of various pavilions, prayer halls, countyards and a group of pagodas dating from the Yuan, Ming and Qing dynasties. These pagodas are tombs of ancient monks and Buddhist masters.

Nestled in the hills, the temple is away from hustles and bustles of the noisy city for both pious devotees and common people who want to relax.

Take a long-distance bus at Zhanlanlu

Open: 8:00-17:00

Temple of Altar (Jietaisi)

Located in Ma'an Hill on the western outskirt of Beijing, the temple has the largest altar to attain full status for a Buddhist monk. The current altar is ten meters in width and length, 3.3 meters in height. The temple is also famed for the ancient pine trees, among which some are over 1,000 years old.

Take a long-distant bus from Zhanlanlu

Open: 8:30-17:30

Fahai Temple

First built in the Ming Dynasty, the temple is now a cultural relic under the state protection.

It preserves 240 square meters of frescos painted by Ming court artists. Completed half a century before Michelangelo began his work on Vatican' Sistine Chapel, the fresco are regarded as masterpieces of religious art worldwide. They portray the guardians of Buddhist scriptures, grotesque animals, and flying fairies.

The modest, peaceful environment in this mountain area has been little affected by the outside world during the past centuries.

The temple is the praying center for Taoist devotees in Beijing.

Buses: 331, 336

White Cloud Taoism Temple (Baiyunguan)

Located outside Xibianmen, the temple dates back to the Tang Dynasty. After a renovation in 1192, the temple was named Palace of Supreme Ultimate (Taijigong). It was totally destroyed by a fire in 1203. During the reign of Shizu of the Yuan Dynasty, a Taoist master named Qiu Chuji rebuilt the temple and was buried here after his death. Since then Taoist adherents have worshipped the temple as an ancestral shrine.

The temple was abandoned through warring years. The disciples of Qiu Chuji rebuilt it again and named it the White Cloud Taoism Temple. Unfortunately, it was burnt down again in the Ming Dynasty. Only in 1706 when Taoism was revived could Taoist monks rebuild this holy place, and gradually expand it as it is today.

The temple is now the location of China Taoism Association.

Bus: 19
Trolley Bus: 114
Open: 8:30-16:30

Niujie Mosque

Islam was brought to China from the Middle East along the Silk Road and through the southern port of Guangzhou.

Muslim Chinese, known as Hui in China, number about 180,000 in Beijing. There are more than 40

mosques to serve them and visiting Muslims. The biggest
are the Niujie Mosque in the old Muslim quarter, and the
Dongsi Mosque, which dates back to the days of Kublai
Khan. The latter has preserved a rare hand-written ver-
sion of Koran of the Yuan Dynasty. Both mosques have
regular worshippers.

    Tel : 3032564

    Bus: 61

    Trolley Bus: 109

The South Cathedral

    Catholicism has a long history in Beijing, where
Jusuit scholar-missionaries like Matteo Ricci, Adam Schall
von Bell and Ferdin and Verbiest were welcomed at the
17th century imperial court for their skills in astronomy
and Western sciences as much as for their Christian mes-
sage.

    The most revered place of worship is the South
Cathedral, built on the site of Ricci's house. The Mass is
held every day at 6:30 am and throughout the morning on
Sunday.

    Tel : 6037139

    Buses: 15, 44

    Trolley Buses: 102, 105, 109

Chapter 3　LIVING IN BEIJING

TELECOMMUNICATIONS & MAIL

In hotels without IDD room service, ring the operator and provide the city and the number you want to call together with your room number and wait for the call back—usually for just a few minutes. This also applies to domestic long distance calls and local calls.

Rates for station to station calls vary according to distance. The average is around $20 (US $ 2.30) per minute with a minimum charge of three minutes. Collect calls are possible only to a few countries but they are cheaper. Hong Kong's calling cards are also accepted in some top hotels and the airport.

Nearly all post offices in Beijing offer local and long distance call service at official rates without any extra service charge. Local calls can also be made at the airport, railway stations or public telephone booths on the street, in the resident's courtyards or apartment blocks. Evidently it is very difficult for foreign visitors to find the latter two locations.

With the constant expansion of Beijing's telecommunications program, many telephone numbers have been changed. In case you fail to get through (especially those of six digits), ask your hotel operator to find out the new number or dial 114 (local directory enquiries).

In addition to the local post offices, there are branch post offices in almost all the tourist hotels in Beijing. According to many foreign resident businessmen, the postal service in Beijing seems more efficient than most countries in the West. An air-mail letter usually takes 4 to 7 days to reach its destination. The postal rates are reasonable if not very cheap. A surface mail letter within China costs 0.20 (US $ 0.03) and 1.50 (US $ 0.15) for overseas. The costs for letters, aerograms and postcards sent by air mail to any place in the world are US $ 0.40, 0.31 and 0. 26 respectively.

For other items such as small packets, printed matters and parcels, you will have to go to the local post offices, because the contents must be checked and sealed there.

International Calls

International calls can be made directly from hotel rooms with IDD phones, by dialing the international prefix '00', plus country code, area code and number. Otherwise call 115 for the international operation service. IDD calls have a one-minute minimum charge. International calls assisted by operators have a minimum of three-minute charge. Hotels usually add a service charge.

Domestic Long-Distance Calls

Direct long-distance calls (DDD) can be made from most hotels to some 2,000 localities in China. Visitors should dial the domestic prefix '0', plus area code and the number. Otherwise callers should dial 173 or 113 for operator-assisted calls. Experienced callers choose the period of 21:00 pm to 7:00 am because it is not only easier to get through but calls are charged half of the daytime price.

City Calls

Calls within the city from a hotel are sometimes charged. Calls from public telephone booths cost two or four 10 fen coins. Most public phones are found in railway stations and shopping centers, where there is an attendant to help make the small change. Calls outside the city can be made from some telephone booths on the street or at a post office throughout the city.

Main Telecommunications Offices

International Post and Telecommunications Office
Yabao Lu, Jianguomen Overpass
Tel : 5128120, 5121114
(Services include post, remittances, money orders and telegraphic money transfers, customs clearance for postal items)

Long Distance
Telephone Building
Fuxingmennei Dajie
Tel : 660941
(IDD, DDD, conference prebooked telephone calls, telegrams, circuit cables)

Telephone Building
Chang'an Jie, Western District
Tel : 664900
(IDD, DDD, fax, telex, telegram. Open 24 hours)

Beijing International Telecommunications Building
Sanyuan Overpass
(A wide range of telecommunications services, with 2, 000 international telephone lines and 12,000 international

telegraph lines)

Mail Delivery

Post offices, with a noteworthy green emblem, are usually located on main streets, railway stations, the airport and major scenic spots. The office hour is from 8:00 am to 5:00 pm, seven days a week. Telegraph, telephone and telex services are available around the clock.

All the hotels have mail boxes for both domestic and international letters. Letters mailed through the boxes with yellow heads can be handled faster than ordinary boxes. No additional stamp is needed.

Phone Cards

The cards are specially issued to offer DDD and IDD services in any directly-dialing phone around the city. Users may buy the cards at Beijing Long-Distance Phonecall Service at Fuxingmen.

Mobile Phone Service

Mobile phones of all brands are useful for busy businessmen.

There are handhold and in-car mobile phones.

Users can dial IDD and DDD, or apply for wandering service in most provincial capitals in China.

International Post & Telecommunications Office

Besides postal services, it handles remittances, money orders, telegraphic money transfer, international and domestic telephone and telegraph services. In the same building is a Customs Office for those needing customs clearance for postal items.

Open: 8:00 am-7:00 pm

Add.: Yabaolu, 300 meters north of Jianguomen Overpass

Tel : 5128114, 5128120

Express Mail Service

EMS, DHL, UPS and TNT provide express postal services for urgent documents, materials and other items to more than 10,000 cities of 170 countries and regions.

Some 45 post offices and express mail counters set in business centers of hotels can also handle the urgent letters. Or you can call 5129947 and 5129948 to ask the staff to pick items at home. Beijing Shuang Chen Express Co. can handle express delivery or send gifts and flowers within the city at customers' request.

DHL-Sinotrans Ltd. 45 Xinguanjie, Chaoyang District

Tel : 466221124 hours service
UPS12 Andinglu
Tel : 4651565

Fax, Telex and Telegram

All major hotels are equipped with these facilities, either in their business center or branch post office. Rates for fax and telex are similar to IDD calls. International telegram rate is 3.50 per word.

HEALTH & MEDICAL SERVICES

China has no specific requirements regarding vaccinations for foreign visitors, provided that you are coming directly from an affected area. Check with your physician or government health authority for their recommendation on vaccinations. For a short visit to Beijing, the possibility of contracting any serious infectious disease is very small. The best prevention is to ensure maximum hygiene.

Hotel rooms are always supplied with thermos flasks of hot and cold boiled water. Few Beijingers drink water from a tap. It would be wise to follow suit. Besides, always wash your hands carefully before each meal and peel the fruit before eating.

There are hundreds of hospitals and medical clinics in Beijing. The following top four are comparable to hospitals in the West, each with a special clinic and an inpatient ward for foreigners.

Beijing Union Hospital
Dongdan, Dongcheng District
Emergency Section
Tel : 5295114

Beijing Hospital
1 Dahualu, Dongcheng District
Tel : 5132266

Friendship Hospital
Yong'anlu, Xuanwu District
Tel : 3014411

Sino-Japanese Friendship Hospital
Heping Jie Beikou, Chaoyang District
Tel : 4221122

Beijing SOS First Aid Center
Qianmen Xidajie
Bilingual Service in Chinese & English
Tel : 6014433

International Medical Center
S 106 Lufthansa Business Center
Tel : 4651561

Hong Kong International Clinic

   3rd Floor of Swissotel Hong Kong Macao Center

   Tel : 5012288 ext 2346

Opinions vary in the West in regard to the traditional Chinese medicine. Those who have experimented with it and the majority of the Chinese people including doctors trained in the West, believe it to be remarkable effective at least for certain illnesses. There are three big Chinese traditional medicine hospitals in Beijing. If you are intersted in trying it out, ask the front desk or the clinic in the hotel to arrange a consultation appointment for you.

Emergency

In case of emergency of any kind, if you are in the hotel, ring the front desk or the security section of the hotel. The following telephone numbers will also be helpful, no matter where you are. It would be a good idea to bring them along with you while in Beijing.

110	Police
119	Fire
120	Ambulance

(Bilingual service in Chinese and English)

   555486   Beijing Public Security Bureau

(Bilingual service in Chinese and English)

   5003419   International SOS First Aid Center

(Bilingual service in Chinese and English)

   5053521   Asian International First Aid Center

(Bilingual service in Chinese and English)

   5051393   European First Aid Center

(Bilingual service in Chinese and English)

   6014336   International Medical Evacuation Office

(Bilingual service in Chinese and English)

SHOPPING

There is a unique feeling about shopping in Beijing that cannot be found anywhere else. Despite the rapid modernization drive encroaching on almost everywhere with its dynamic pace, some of the old, unusual and exciting hutongs (side streets) with their mysterious siheyuans (courtyards) remain intact in this splendid city.

Strolling around the old streets, just let your imagination run wild with what it must have looked like in ancient times, by then the camel caravans arrived to the city gates and unloaded exotic spices and other goods brought from faraway places.

The camels are long gone from the city streets. Almost anything, whether produced by Chinese or Western, is available. The shops and boutiques in joint venture hotels are full of soft cashmere and silk, while a wide variety of Chinese arts and crafts beckon the travelers to purchase.

PLACES TO SHOP

Wangfujing Dajie

Just around the corner from Beijing Hotel, is the most fashionable and perhaps the busiest shopping area with large department stores, bookstores, large and small arts and crafts shops, and Western boutiques one after another along two sides of the street, including the Beijing Department Store, a new Benetton and the Hong Kong owned Concord Department Store, the Beijing Arts and Crafts Shop and the Beijing Paintings Shop. A gigantic renovation project is now underway.

Qianmen Dajie and Dashilan

The area to the south of Tian'anmen Square has been a commercial center for five centuries, overflowing with traditional shops. It is a favorite shopping area for local residents, with stores such as the 400-year-old Liubiju Pickles Shop, Yueshengzhai which is famous for its stewed beef, the Tongrentang Drug Store, the oldest pharmacy that uses secret recipes of the Qing court, the Ruifuxiang Clothing Store, and the Qianxiangyi Seasoning Store.

Xidan

North of west Chang'an Dajie, the street provides a wide range of shopping options. At one end is the Xidan Market, famous for cheap clothing and the World of Nationalities, where you can find costumes from various minority areas. There is the new Xidan Shopping Center, with two floors packed with high-quality goods, from electrical appliances to imported fashion.

Dongsi Commercial Area

The market place in the middle of Wangfujing Street was developed from an old fair around Longfu Temple. Here you will find shops of every size. The Longfu Building is one of Beijing's four biggest department stores. There are also many privately-owned street stalls.

Silver Street

At Dongdan Beidajie, the shopping street has many boutiques selling imported products.

Shopping Centers

To avoid the always over-crowded commercial districts, tourists can also go shopping at arcades of major hotels and newly erected shopping centers.

In addition, there are dozens of stores designated by

Beijing Tourism Administration, including the Friendship
Store, to serve overseas travelers. They are ideal shopping places to buy arts and crafts, antiques and other Beijing specialties. Postal and consigning services are available.

Today, Beijing residents enjoy the convenience and
luxury of shopping at one shop for everything from local
specialties to international brand-name products. Walking
into any of the dozen biggest shopping arcades, one real-
izes that shopping is no longer a hardship but a pleasure
and relaxation so long as you have enough to spend.

Bejing-Lufthansa Friendship Shopping City
 52 Liangmaqiao, Chaoyang District

CVIK-Yaohan shopping Center22 Jianwai Dajie

Guiyou Shopping Mall
 5A Jianwai Dajie

Blue Island Building
 8 Chaowai Dajie, Chaoyang District

Urban-Rural Trade Center
 23 Fuxinglu

Parkson Shopping Center
 North of the Fuxingmen Overpass

Concorde Department Store
 192 Chaonei Dajie

WHAT TO BUY?

Antiques

As the capital of six dynasties, Beijing attracts antique-seekers around the world. The ideal shopping place for curio virtuosos is the Liulichang Cultural Street, the restored "Culture Street" of the Qing Dynasty. It sells everything from small artistic items to old books and antiques.

The name of Liulichang means Glazed Tile Workshop when it served as the official glazed tile kiln for the construction of the Forbidden City. Later it became a favorite place for scholars and artists who sought for old books and curios sold by improverished gentries in the early 20th century.

Rongbaozhai Studio offers paintings and calligraphic works by renowned Chinese artists. The China Bookstore binds and repairs all kinds of old books and periodicals, and sells them. Coins cast in different dynasties can be found in the Coin Store. The antique stores and its branches deal with porcelain, cloisonne, jade and replicas of Ming and Qing dynasties furniture.

All the buildings imitate the architectural styles of the late Qing Dynasty. Among the most sought-after antiques are blue-and-white porcelain, calligraphic scrolls, paintings, jade ornaments, old costumes, and furniture. In addition to Liulichang, antiques are also sold in the Friendship Store and hotel arcades.

Antiques that date before 1795 under Qing Emperor Qianlong's reign cannot be sold or exported. Those made after the date should bear a small red seal from BCRB to indicate they can be taken out of the country. The seal also proves the genuineness of the items. The receipts indicate the name and age of the antiques if these items are bought in the designated stores.

Recently, the BCRB approved the operation of six curio markets to conduct antique business. These markets are bargain lovers' paradise, as bargaining is an ancient tradition which is more treated as an art. Nobody will be offended. Buyers are suggested to cut 50% below the offered price, then be ready to make concessions, preparing to pay at a little higher price than what you had offered.

Silk

The silks that have brought fame to China can be readily found, in a dazzling array of colors, patterns and textures.

High quality silk and silk products can be bought in large shopping centers and arcades in hotels. The Xiushui and Yabaolu markets sell various kinds of silk skirts, underwear, and bedspreads. Most vendors are self-employed people who speak some English. But they are flexible in business, and travelers can bargain over the prices. All the products are in Western size.

Carpets

Carpets, modern and antique, for use as tapestries or rugs, are plentiful and bargain priced. Those made in Beijing are close-woven with fine wool cut into sharp, elegant patterns, such as the famous dragon and phoenix design.

Medicine

Chinese drugstores sell various kinds of nutritious pills and tonics made from herbs. Tongrentang and other traditional pharmacies have a "resident" doctor feeling pulse and making prescription.

All the large department stores and supermarkets have special drug counters.

Books

Every year 20,000 titles and 1,300 periodicals are published in Beijing. The city is the home of the Commercial Press and other well known publishing houses. They make up a small part of the stock of the city's major book stores, where you can find beautiful art books, translations of Chinese classics, and textbooks on all subjects. Price is reasonable.

The Beijing Foreign Language Bookstore and the Beijing Xinhua Bookstore (with 137 branches around the town) are major book sellers.

Shopping Tips

1. Shops open seven days a week, from 8:30 am to 8:00 pm (7:00 pm in winter). Large shopping centers and the Friendship Store may stay open to 9:00 pm and offer more Westernized ambience. Night marts usually begin their business at twilight.

2. For foreign buyers, the safest places to shop are those shops designated by Beijing Tourism Administration, where one can always feel easy about the price and quality of goods and can find a money exhange desk. Anyone who wishes to try bargaining with vendors had better change his money in advance.

3. Keep all purchase receipts in case you might to return or exchange your purchases. Bargaining is only possible with private vendors in these street stalls which may not allow refund or change even if the quality is unthinkably low. So be careful.

SHOPPING LIST

Antiques

Beijing Friendship Store
17 Jianguomenwai Dajie
Tel : 5003311

Huaxia Arts & Crafts Store
Dongdan
Tel : 5247307

Huaxia Arts & Crafts
Branch Store
293 Wangfujing Dajie
Tel : 5251819

Curio Markets
Haiwang Village Curio Market (on Liulichang Street)
Liulichang Xingyi Studio (behind the Rongbaozhai Studio)
Hongqiao Market (North Gate of Temple of Heaven)
Jinsong Curio & Antique Market (on South Third Ring Road)
Chaowai Curio Market (North of Ritan Park)
Shichahai Market (at the north gate of Beihai Park)
Huangchenggen Market (shatan, Dongcheng District)

HANDICRAFTS AND JEWELRY

Beijing Friendship
Store
17 Jianguomenwai Dajie
Tel : 5003311

Beijing Arts & Crafts
Branch Store
265 Wangfujing Dajie
Tel : 5127691

White Peacock Arts
and Crafts World
Dewai Beibinhelu
Tel : 2011199

Beijing Jade Factory
Foreign Service Center
11 Guangminglu,
Chaoyang District
Tel : 707371 Ext.371

China Arts & Crafts Trading & Exhibition Co.
5 Xinwai dajie
Tel : 2025857

Gift Palace of Huacui Beijing Exhibition Center
Tel : 8316677 Ext.4243

Landmark Shopping
Arcade
Bei Sanhuandonglu
Tel : 5016688-5678

CHINESE CALLIGRAPHY AND PAINTING

Rongbaozhai
19 Xi Liulichang

Beijing Painting &
Calligraphy Shop
289 Wangfujing Dajie

Yanhuang Art Gallery
9 Asian Games Village
Tel : 4911046

Wangfu Painting &
Calligraphy Shop
67 Wangfujing Dajie
Tel : 5133629

Yanjing Painting & Callig-
raphy
House, Qiniandian Branch
Inside the Tiantan Park
Tel : 7025262

SILK

Yuanlong Embroidery
& Silk Company
55 Tiantanlu, Chongwen
District
Tel : 7012854

Beijing International
Embroidery & Silk Store
402 Anhuili,
Anwai Dajie
Tel : 4914185

Beijing Silk Store

Beijing Friendship Store

5 Zhubaoshi, Qianmen
Dajie
call 3016658

Beijing Ruifuxiang Silk
Store
5 Dashalan, Qianmen

17 Jianguomenwai
Dajie
Tel : 5003311

CARPETS

Beijing Carpet Trade
Center
90 Weizikeng,
Liangjiazhuang
Tel : 7616018

Marco Polo Carpet
Store
2/f China World Shopping
Arcade
Tel : 5051974

Beijing-Lufthansa
Youyi Shopping City
52 Liangmaqiaolu
Tel : 4651188

Huaxia Arts & Crafts
Branch Store
293 Wangfujing
Dajie
Tel : 5251819

FURNITURE

Replicas of ancient furiture and antique furniture:

Beijing Chinese-Fashioned
Furniture Factory
64 Yongdingmenwai Dajie
Tel : 7223344

Weiyi Mahgony Furniture

White Peacock Arts
and Crafts World
Dewai Beibinhelu
Tel : 2011199

Beijing Friendship Store

City
37 Dongjiaominxiang

17 Jianguomenwai Dajie
Tel : 5003311

Family-use and Office Furniture :
CVIK-Yaohan Shopping
Center
22 Jianguomenwai
Dajie
Tel : 5124488

Yihua Furniture
City
Dabeiyao Overpass,
Jianwai Dajie
Tel : 5089298

Sanyou Furniture World
Military Museum,
9 Fuxinglu
Tel : 8514357

FOOD

Wellcome Supermarket in
China World Trade Center

Lido Supermarket
in Holiday Inn Lido Hotel

CVIK Supermarket

Youyi Shopping City

TOYS

New China Children's
Store
17 Wangfujing Dajie

Wangfujing Department
Store
255 Wangfjujing Dajie

Xinshidai Children's Store
Dashilan, Qianmen

China World Trade Center
1 Jianguomenwai Dajie

MEDICINE

Tongrentang Drugstore
24 Dashilan, Xuanwu
District
Tel : 3032871

Wangfujing Drugstore
267 Wangfujing
Dajie
Tel : 5252322

BOOKS

Wangfujing Foreign
Language Bookstore
Wangfujing Dajie

Xidan Foreign Language
Store
Xidan

BEAUTY SALOON

Beijing now has beauty saloons up to western standards. All located inside hotels and large shopping centers or in major commercial areas and diplomatic compound.

Silian Beauty Saloon
Tel : 5255281

Swan Beauty Center
Tel : 4663311-3833

Queen Beauty Center
Tel : 5257059, 5126865

Liren Beauty salon
Tel : 5150358/
5052288-2182

Beijing Windsor Beauty
Salon
Tel : 5126321

Roger Craig
China World Hotel
Tel : 5052266/5128899

Natural Beauty
Tel : 3175236

Huan Sha Beauty Salon
Tel : 6011602

CHINESE GOWN TAILOR

Chinese long gown is considered the most elegant garment most suitable for women's figures. Following are two suggested tailors to make Chinese gowns.

Gown shop for celebrities	Mingxing Clothe Store
12 Dongdan Beidajie	Wangfujing Dajie
Tel : 5224936	Tel : 5257945

DINING

Dining in China has long been looked upon as a pleasure and a cultural experience. In Beijing alone, a plethora of tasty dishes awaits both the adventurous and hungry travelers.

There are thousands of eating places in Beijing, serving more than half a dozen different Chinese cuisine. Thanks to the proliferation of modern hotels, the city now also boasts restaurants that prepare food from all parts of the world. One can taste genuine French, Russian and American cuisine, as well as Japanese, Korean and Thai food cooked by native chefs. There are also outlets for the world's most popular fast food, such as McDonald's and Pizza Hut.

Hotels serve some of the best meals and have the best service. Local restaurants are more crowded and noisier, but they portray a fuller sense of local flavor. Lunch is between 10 am and 2 pm, and dinner is traditionally from 6 to 8 pm. However, dining habits are changing and more restaurants stay open after 9 pm. It is best to telephone abead to book seats.

The best known places have bilingual Chinese-English menus. And usually there are English-speaking waiters. Visitors can use credit cards or travelers' cheques in restaurnts within hotels.

Sometimes eating out can create a new entertainment and taste, especially when sampling such Beijing snacks as dumplings, noodles and family-style dishes. The ambience is more family-like.

Those who are allergic to gourmet powder had better remind the chef in advance.

CHINESE COOKERY

Beijing Cuisine

Many of the dishes classified as "Beijing" style originated in the Imperial court, which had at its command the best of all the food of China.

Beijing cuisine makes liberal use of stronger flavored roots and vegetables such as peppers, garlic, ginger, leek and coriander (Chinese parsley). Because of its more northerly location, the food of Beijing tends to be more substantial, to keep the body warm. Instead of rice, which is the staple diet of the southerners, more noodles, dumplings, and bread (baked, steamed or fried) are served in Beijing style restaurants. Demonstrations of the highly skilled art of turning a lump of dough into a skein of even-sized noodles can be observed in some restaurants.

The most famous dish is Beijing Roast Duck, usually prepared for a minimum of six people, of which the crisp skin is the most prized part. To achieve such crispness, the duck is air-dried, then coated with a mixture of syrup and soy sauce before roasting. When ready, it is presented ceremoniously and the skin deftly carved. These pieces are wrapped in thin pancakes with onions or leeks, cucumber, turnip and plum sauce. Upon request, the remainder of the duck meat can be sauteed with bean sprouts, and the bones made into a wonderful soup with cabbage.

Hot pot is also a favorite dish for foreigners. People gather around the pot, dip slices of mutton in the boiling water for a while, then eat the mutton with a specially made sauce. The best restaurants are the age-long Donglaishun, and Youyishun.

Court Cuisine

Two restaurants offer meals fit for an emperor, in brilliantly-restored rooms where once the court of the Qing Dynasty used to dine. They are Fangshan, set below the White Pagoda of Beihai Park, and Tingliguan, literally "Listening to the Orioles Pavilion", formerly a theater in the Summer Palace. There are others specializing in the sumptuous banquets of a dozen or so courses. One is Li Jia Cai, run by the daughter of a former court chef.

Sichuan Cuisine

The food of China's largest province is distinguished by the clever use of spices, resulting in dishes that usually taste hot. Their distinctive flavor is culinary evidence of the mountainous province's long geographical isolation. The fascinating variety and subtle use of flavoring additives in the region's cuisine helps to explain its appeal. One favorite starter with many visitors is a dish of curling, crisp, super-thin slices of beef impregnated with the truly tangy peel of "gulden orange" (kumquat).

Chicken, pork, fresh water fish and shellfish are all popular ingredients. Rice gets a very special Sichuan treatment in "crackling" or "crispy" rice dishes, in which the deep-fried dried scrapping from the bottom of the rice pan are covered with a rich, spicy sauce of seafood, meat or vegetables. The resulting sound effects are a culinary chorus of "snap, crackle and pop".

The largest restaurant serving Sichuan dishes is in Sichuan Hotel, while the smaller but more delicate is the Dou Hua Zhuang Restaurant.

Cantonese Cuisine

Cantonese cuisine is known for its fresh and delicate flavors. Freshly bought ingredients are prepared the same day and cooked just before serving, using little oil or spicy seasonings.

Seafood is so fresh that it hardly touches dry land before it arrives on your dinner table. In many seafood restaurants, you can actually choose your own fish from the tank in which they swim.

Frozen and processed foods are not usually found in Chinese kitchens. However, dried seafood, like shark's fin, abalone and scallop, are often used.

Dim sum, a special Cantonese snack not to be missed, is served in many Cantonese restaurants.

Chaozhou Cuisine

Chaozhou is reputed for its seafood cooking, which creates unforgettable fresh flavors. The mouth-watering prawns, oysters, crabs and eels, combined with family-style pickles, play a symphony of traditional cuisine.

The ingredients, such as the shark's fin and edible bird's nest, are cooked in a unique way with special seasoning juice. Famous dishes include salt-baked goose with vinegar juice, steamed shrimp with orange juice, and fish rice with bean sauce. A tea ceremony is held during the service of dishes, not just for show but good for digest.

The Carrianna Chiu Chow Restaurant serves genuine

Chaozhou cuisine in Beijing.

Jiangsu Cuisine

The most famed restaurant of Jiangsu style is Yu Hua Tai Restaurant which has operated since 1921. Its eel banquet and various snacks are very good. It is also famous for West Lake fish and Beggar's Chicken, both Hangzhou dishes. The chicken is baked in lotus leaves and clay.

Beggar's chicken was actually invented by a Hangzhou thief, as legends put it. Because the thief had no stove, he wrapped the stolen bird in clay and baked it in a hole in the ground.

Shanghai Cuisine

Shanghai, a major seaport at the estuary of the Yangtze River, does not really have a cuisine of its own, but successfully refines all the work of the surrounding provinces. The flavors are generally richer, heavier, sweeter and oilier than those of Cantonese Cuisine.

More use is made of preserved vegetables and pickles, and salted meat is a feature. Lime-and-ginger-flavored "100-year-old" eggs are perhaps Shanghai's best-known culinary preservation work. Its best-known delicacy is "hairy crab". Other popular dishes include "eight treasure" duck, "drunken" chicken, braised eel and sweet-and-sour croaker.

Shandong Cuisine

The cuisine of neighboring Shandong Province is a dominant part in Beijing's home cooking. The restaurants of the city serving it outnumber all others. Thanks to its long coastline the province excels in fish and seafood dishes, such as sea cucumber, "squirrel fish", jumbo prawns, crab and eel. Among Shandong restaurants are the

Fengzeyuan and Kongshantang, or Hall of Confucian Food on Liulichang Cultural Street, where deep fried scorpion is a seasonal specialty.

Shanxi Cuisine

The cuisine of this northern province is noted for its crisp duck, deep-fried pork and a variety of wheaten dishes. The biggest Shanxi restaurant in Beijing is Jinyang on Zhushikou Dajie, in an imposing building that was once the residence of Ji Xiaolan, a leading scholar of the Qing Dynasty.

Hunan Cuisine

Sometimes called Xiang Cuisine, Hunan's culinary specialties are akin to those of the chili-rich Sichuan dishes. Chili, garlic and an unusual sauce called "strange-flavor" sauce on some menus, enliven many dishes. Sweetness, too, is a Hunanese culinary passion, and honey sauce often goes with desserts such as water chestnut or cassia flower cakes.

Rice is Hunan's staple, but northern-style side dishes and fillers are also popular: beancurd "bread" rolls or dumplings and savory buns. They are a sign that Hunan is one of China's culinary heartland, incorporating many flavors and regional influences.

Korean Cuisine

Many Beijingers like the spicy taste of Korean dog meat noodle, dog meat soup, roast fish, and pickles. Yanji Restaurant, located on Xisi Dajie, Sorabol Restaurant in Landmark Hotel and Arirang in VCIK Club offer genuine Korean dishes.

Xinjiang Cuisine

Turpan Restaurant is a popular venue for sampling

the exotic cuisine of far western Xinjiang. A featured dish is a whole roast lamb cooked by a famous Uygur chef.

Mongolian Cuisine

Mongolian cooking specializes in roast beef and mutton. In Xilin Guole Restaurant and Genghis Khan Restaurant, visitors can try a taste of the grassland, such as roast lamb leg. Diners may have a special roast mutton dish eaten with their fingers as Mongolian do.

Muslim Cuisine

Beijing has a large number of Muslim residents. Muslim restaurants enjoy a brisk business. The age-long restaurants, such as Hongyunlou and Hongbinlou, offer delicious Muslim and vegetarian dishes.

Tonic Food

According to traditional Chinese medicine, those dishes cooked with ginseng, pilose antler, bear's paw, soft-shelled turtle and the fruit of Chinese wolfberry are both delicious and nutritious. The Longhua Tonic Food restaurant and Xiyuan Yangsheng Studio are reputed dining place for tonic foods.

Snacks

Chinese snacks are so many they can constitute a cuisine of their own. A lovely snack market open for lunch and dinner lines the southwest shore of Front Lake, immediately north of the north gate of Beihai Park.

A special tourist-type night market, clean and yet inexpensive, has been set up in a large courtyard next to Peace Hotel (Wangfujing Street) and Changliang Square between Great Wall Sheraton Hotel and Landmark Towers, Liangmahe Hotel.

Two more transient markets for traditional snacks

operate in Donghuamen Street (next to East Gate of the Forbidden City) and Dongsi Night Market on Dongsi Street.

Hot Pot

It is one of the favorites for Beijingers in winter. The traditional Mongolian hot pot is now joined by Cantonese- and Sichuan-style hot pots. The ingredients for hot pots of different styles are mainly beef, mutton, seafood and vegetables. The stock of Cantonese is light in taste, while the Sichuan hot pot features hot and spicy stock to enhance flavor.

Fast Food

Western and Chinese fast-food is a rising star in Beijing. McDonald's, Kentucky Fried Chicken and Pizza Hut have been widely accepted by Beijing people, especially the young.

Nostalgia Cuisine

It is also called "cultural revolution cuisine" by some foreigners. The eateries, named after the old revolutionary slogans, such as Black Earth, Old Three Grades, offer a culinary trip back to China in the '60s and '70s. These dining places are more like venues "in memory of things past" for those nostalgic urban youth of the time.

Drinks

In restaurants and bars you will find European and Chinese grape wines; beers from China (including the famous Tsingtao), Hong Kong and Japan; imported and domestic spirits (Chinese vodka is excellent); and Chinese traditional drinks such as the very powerful Maotai and less potent Shaoxing rice wine. Bottled mineral water and Coco Cola are also available.

There are small private bars opening around the city at frequent intervals, however they close just as often. These bars cater to the taste of youth, while the elderly still prefer to sip tea in the traditional teahouses.

Coming to Grips With chopsticks

If you really want to enjoy eating Chinese food, you should learn to use chopsticks properly.

1. Rest the first chopstick in the gap between your first finger and your thumb, hold it firmly by pressing the lower joint of your thumb against the tip of your third finger. Remember that this stick should always remain fixed.

2. Then grap the second stick between the tips of your first and second fingers and the ball of your thumb.

3. To pick up food, always move the upper stick with your third and second fingers while the lower one remains unmoved.

4. Practise to see how far up the chopsticks should be held. Usually the tip of your third finger is just at the middle of your chopsticks.

AMUSEMENT PARKS

Beijing Amusement Park

Longtanhu Park, Chongwen District
Covering 18 hectares with 19 amusement programs
Open: 9:00-18:00
Tel: 7011155
Buses: 6,12,41,64

Miyun International Amusement Park

Miyun County
Offering 20 amusement programs, including on-wa-

ter ballroom and game rooms.

> Open: 8:30-16:30 (from April to October)
> Tel: 9943585

Nine-Dragon Amusement Park

> Ming Tombs Reservoir

The largest underwater amusement park in Asia. Rides through classcal buildings, with robots, lights and special audio-visual effects, to reveal ancient Chinese legends.

> Open: 8:30-16:30
> Tel: 9472164
> Bus: 912

Shijingshan Amusement Park

> Shijingshan District
> 40 amusement programs
> Open: 9:00-16:45
> Tel: 8874060
> Buses: 337, 307

CCTV Tower

> Xisanhuan Zhonglu, Haidian District

The Central Radio & TV Tower is Asia's second tallest structure. Visitors, within 60 seconds, can go up to the tower-top 238 meters above the ground. Visitors can have a grand view below and enjoy a full meal in the circular restaurant.

> Tel: 8475807

CULTURAL LIFE

Beijing has more than 100 institutions of higher learning, 70 museums and residences of late celebrities, the largest library in Asia, and TV stations. Ballet, acrobatics and Western music as well as other kinds of Chinese and foreign shows are active in the capital.

Life of Beijing residents is a combination of ancient traditions and modern rhythms. Peking Opera co-exists with Western ballet and symphonies. While young pop fans cheer their idols from Hong Kong, the elderly gather under the shadow of trees in the front yards of sidestreets to play chess and sip tea.

The people of Beijing spare no efforts to preserve fine national traditions. Meanwhile, they are eagerly absorbing new knowledge to enrich their life.

FESTIVALS

As a city with a long history and a melting pot of Chinese ethnic groups, the people of Beijing observe many festive celebrations the year round. Besides some traditional festivals such as the Spring Festival and the New Year's Day, several new folklore festivals are observed, such as Kite Festival in spring, Water Melon Festival in summer and Smoke Leave Festival in autumn.

Spring Festival

The Spring Festival (also known as the Lunar New Year), which falls in late January or early February, is a national festival.

In old times the coming of a New Year meant a time to settle debts and quarrels, a visit to the fortune teller, sacrifice to ancestors and the Kitchen God who was supposed to report to the Jade Emperor on the family's conduct during the past year at the end of each year. The old customs have much been abandoned. But the festival is still a great occasion for family reunions and special food.

The children are given little red packets containing some money (yasuiqian)—the color red meaning lucky.

In the weeks before the festival, sales are brisk and streets and markets are festooned with colorful lanterns. Although fireworks are banned in Beijing, temple fairs (miaohui) in which visitors are entertained by local performances attract more and more sightseers from home and abroad.

Mid-Autumn Festival

Traditionally this was a harvest festival, but it also had a political significance. During an uprising against the ruling Mongol Yuan Dynasty in the 14th century, messages were passed to conspirators in moon cakes. Today these cakes no longer contain messages, but a large variety of sweet and savory fillings. The mixture includes pork, duck egg, lotus seeds, sugar and red beans.

New Year's Day

The two-day holiday is celebrated much like the Spring Festival in China but on a much lesser scale.

National Day

Except the Spring Festival, the National Day, on October 1, is the most important holiday in China.

During celebrations of the National Day, Beijing is elaborately decorated. Streets are lined with flowers and colorful flags, and red lanterns are hung in front of shops and official buildings. A National Day reception and performance are held in the Great Hall of the People while various kinds of performances and local operas are shown at all theaters. At night, when neons lights are on throughout the city, families have a fine chance to enjoy the night scene out in the street.

A grand parade or a mass demonstration is usually

held in every fifth or tenth anniversary.

Folklore Events for Tourists

Ice Lantern Festival at Longqing Gorge is held in January or February each year. Ice sculptures are carved out of thick blocks of ice with colorful lanterns inside, shaping an icy wizard of OZ.

Dragon Pond Fair

Folk performances from all parts of Beijing are gathered in the Dragon Pond (Longtan) Park to compete for excellence.

Ditan Fair

The temple fair follows traditions of the Ming and Qing dynasties, in which the God of Earth s worshipped and folk performances played.

Fair at Big Bell Temple

Visitors can strike the big bell during the Spring Festival for three times in morning, noon and evening. All who listen to the sound are blessed by the God of Bell in the coming year, as local legend puts it.

Smoke Leaves Festival

Many smoke trees and Chinese sweet gums grow on the Fragrant Hills. Around the Frost's Descent (18th solar term) each year, the tree leaves turn red, unfolding colorful scenery in autumn, the best season in Beijing.

Dragon Boat Race

Dragon boat race is organized at the Summer Palace, Dragon Pond Park and the Ming Tombs Reservoir around the Dragon Boat Festival (5th day of the fifth lunar month). The race is a ritual in memory of Qu Yuan, a great poet in pre-Christ times.

Water Melon Festival
   Water melons grown in Panggezhuang of Daxing
County are the most sweet and tasty. To celebrate the
harvest of water melons, the county organizes a festival
each year in which visitors can pick melons themselves in
the fields and enjoy folk performances.

Double Ninth Festival
   It is a traditional festival on the 9th day of the 9th
lunar month. People usually go hiking, climb mountains,
enjoy blooming chrysanthemum and prepare special cakes
for the festival. It is also an occasion for the elderly to get
together.

Beijing International Kite Festival
   An annual event in Mentougou District in spring.

NIGHT LIFE

   Most night life venues are in downtown area around
joint venture hotels. Almost every four or five-star hotel
has now a facility where people can dance or sing along
the music, either live, or with a karaoke machine. Outside the hotels there are some night spots that stay open
till midnight or later and offer live music, dancing, and
karaoke.
   The following are some night life programs.

Twilight in Tian'anmen Square
   Visitors can take a rickshaw along Chang'an Av-
enue, the widest street in the world, to Tian'anmen
Square. Then enter on foot through the Gate of Heavenly

Peace and across the Golden Water Bridge to Wumen Square, the front yard of the Forbidden City. After strolling along the eastern moat of the imperial palaces, you can take a taxi from Wangfujing to your hotel.

Folklore Performance

Theaters, such as the Lao She Teahouse, Tianqiao Happy Teahouse, and Liyuan theater, offer a large repertoire of traditional performance, including Peking Opera and other folklore arts, which date centuries ago. Visitors can enjoy the show over a cup of specially made tea and snacks.

Night Marts

Special tourist-type night markets, clean and inexpensive, have been set up next to Beijing Hotel, Palace Hotel, Minzu Hotel and in Changliang Square between Great Wall Sheraton Hotel and Landmark Tower. Never miss the chance to enjoy the delicious snacks of old Beijing.

Recreational Centers

Recreational centers offer swimming, sauna, massage, dancing, bowling and other programs through out the night. KaraokeDisco Karaoke and disco halls inside and outside hotels throughout the town stay open till midnight or later.

Nightclubs

Nightclubs are ideal places for businesspeople after busy negotiations.

Their interior is lavishly decorated with live music, a spacious ballroom and luxurious KTV rooms.

PLACES FOR NIGHT LIFE

Folk Art Show

Tianqiao Happy Teahouse
113 Tianqiao Market
Open: 9:00-14:30,
       19:00-21:00
Tel: 3040617

Lao She Teahouse
3/F, Da Wan Cha Bdg.
3 Qianmen Xidajie
Open: 19:30-21:30
Tel: 3036830

Peking Opera

Liyuan Theater
Qianmen Hotel
Open: 19:15-21:30
Tel: 3016688 ext 8860

Acrobatic Show

Chaoyang Theater
36 Dongsanhuan Beilu
Hujialou
Open: 19:15-20:30
Tel: 5072421

Erqi Theater
15 Erqijuchang Lu
Fuxingmenwai Dajie
19:15-20:30
Tel: 8526262

Disco

Glass Room
Kunlun Hotel
Open: 19:00-02:30
Tel: 5003388

Jungle
Tianlun Dynasty Hotel
20:00-02:00
Tel: 5138888 ext 8055

House Ballroom
Peace Hotel
Open: 20:30-02:00
Tel: 5128833 ext 6622

Brilliant
East Gate of Worker's
Sports Center
Sanlitun
Tel: 5085845

NASA
SQ2, Xi Tucheng Haidian
District
Tel : 2016622 ext 231,
       2032906

JJDsco
74-76 Xinjiekou
Beidajie
Tel : 6079395, 6079691

Shunfeng Star River
16 Dongsanhuan Lu
Tel : 5071447

Nightman Disco
2 Xibahe Nanli
Tel : 4662382

Song & Dance Hall
Media Center
Open: 19:30-00:30
Tel : 8514422

Talk of the Town
China World Hotel
21:30-02:00
Tel : 5052266 ext 6126

Karaoke

Galaxy
Jianguo Hotel
Open: 20:00-00:00
Tel : 5002233

Lost Horizon
China World Hotel
19:00-01:00
Tel : 5052266 ext 6569

Golden Palace
New Century Hotel
Open: 20:00-02:00

Moving Cloud
Capital Hotel
20:00-00:00

Saga Club
Grand Hotel Beijing
Open: 20:00-02:00
Tel : 5137788 ext 567

Paradise Club
Holiday Inn Crown Plaza
20:00-02:00
Tel : 5133388 ext 1194

The Point After
Palace Hotel
Open: 20:00-03:00
Tel : 5128899 ext 7922

Rainbow
Grace Hotel
19:00-01:00
Tel : 4362288 ext 2610

Top One
Landmark Tower
Open: 20:00-02:00
Tel: 5016688 ext 2688

Xanadu
Shangri-La Hotel
Open: 20:00-02:00
Tel: 8412211 ext 2725

Xianchi Ballroom
Inter-Continental Hotel
Open: 20:00-01:00
Tel: 4915588

Lily
Exhibition
Open: 19:30-02:00

Galary Disco
China Resources Hotel
Open: 20:00-01:00
Tel: 5012233 ext 303

Moonlight
Jing Guang Center
Open: 20:30-01:00
Tel: 5018888

Hualin
Xinqiao Hotel
Open: 19:00-02:00
Tel: 5133366 ext 1348

Meuoy
Taiwan Hotel
21:00-02:00
Tel: 5136688

Yeming Zhu
Media Center
Open: 20:00-02:00
Tel: 8514422 ext 1606

Singing Lounge
CVIK Hotel
Open: 20:00-01:00
Tel: 5123388 ext 2234

Dynasty
Guangdong Regency Hotel
Open: 20:00-02:30

Sakura
Beijing Hotel
Open: 13:00-02:00
Tel: 5137766 ext 1376

Star Light
Tiantan Hotel
Open: 20:00-02:00
Tel: 7012277 ext 2397

Recreational Centers

Apollo Amusement
City
Friendship Hotel
Open: 24 hours service
Tel: 8498298

Beijing Recreational Center
Asian Games Village
Open: 9:30-00:00
Tel: 4993434

Beijing International
Health Land
12 Xinyuanli Dongjie
Open: 24 hours service
Tel: 4661302

Clubs

Fu Hua Celebrities Club
39 Xingfu Dajie
Tel: 7023936, 7026619

Fica International
Gymnastic Club
2 Gongti Beilu Xinzhongjie
Tel: 5088515, 5088516

Royal International
Club
Changguan Lu,
Xizhimen
Tel: 8338112

Capital Club
Capital Mansion
Tel: 4669098

Countryside Club
1 Guan Zhuang
Tel: 5765511

Success Club
4 Gongti Donglu
Tel: 5006362

Tian Yuan Recreation City
Andingmen Wai
Tel: 4251666, 4251188

Antina Beauty & Fitness
Centre
56 Xiaoguan,
Dongzhimenwai Xijie
Tel: 4617038

New Classical Club
Olympic Center
Tel: 4910938, 4910951

Olympic Athletic Club
Swissotel
Tel: 5012288 ext 2305

Nightclubs

Catwalk
Jingguang Centre
Open: 20:00-02:00
Tel : 5018075

Casablanca
Urban-Rural Trade Center
Open: 19:30-02:00
Tel : 8216911

Top Ten
21 Dongxi Shitiao
Open: 20:00-03:00
Tel : 4013388

The Eden Club
3/f, West Wing of
Poly Bdg.
Open: 20:00-02:00
Tel : 5011281

King Star
Mandrin Hotel
Open: 20:00-03:00
Tel : 8319988 ext 15618

Cyclone Fun Pub
Holiday Inn Lido Hotel
Tel : 4376688

Cafe & Bar

Aladding's Hideaway
Tianlun Dynasty Hotel
Open: 23:00-01:00
Tel : 5138888 ext 8163

Derby
Swissotel
Open: 20:00-02:00
Tel : 5012288

Brauhaus
China World Trade Center
Open: 23:00-01:00
Tel : 5052266 ext 6565

Gallery
Holiday Inn Lido Hotel
Open: 23:00-01:00
Tel : 4376688 ext 1956

The Caravan
Great Wall Sheraton Hotel
Open: 23:00-01:00
Tel : 5005566

Hard Rock Cafe
Landmark Hotel
Open: 11:30-00:00
Tel : 5016688 ext 2571

Charlie's

Hollywood East

Jianguo Hotel
Open: 12:30-00:30
Tel: 5002233

Kunlun Hotel
Open: 18:00-00:00
Tel: 5003388

Peacock Bar
Shangri-La Hotel
Open: 18:00-02:00
Tel: 8412211 ext 2723

Inn Bar
Holiday Inn Crown Plaza
Open: 23:30-01:00
Tel: 5133388 ext 1108

Pig and Whistle
Holiday Inn Lido Hotel
Open: 17:00-01:00
Tel: 5136688

Iexas
Taiwan Hotel
Open: 15:00-23:00
Tel: 4376688 ext 1976

Showcase
Gloria Plaza
Open: 21:30-00:00
Tel: 5158855

Grassland
Media Center
Open: 16:00-00:00
Tel: 8514422

Silk
Chang Fu Gong Hotel
Open: 17:30-01:00
Tel: 5125555

Spruse Goose
Movenpick Hotel
Open: 17:00-02:00
Tel: 4565588 ext 1419

Tea Lounge
Grand Hotel
Open: 10:00-21:00
Tel: 5137788 ext 345

Fountain
Grand Hotel
10:00-00:00
Tel: 5137788 ext 349

Apricot
Xi Yuan Hotel
Open: 10:00-01:30
Tel: 8313388 ext 112

Club Bar
China World Hotel
17:00-01:00
Tel: 5052266 ext 36

Captain Nemo

Fairyland

New Century Hotel
Open: 17:00-01:00
Tel: 8492001 ext 35051

Continental Grand Hotel
Open: 20:00-02:00
Tel: 4915588 ext 72159

Pimm's
Hilton Hotel
Tel: 4662288 ext 7340

THE THEATER

Peking Opera

With a history of 200 years, Peking Opera has influenced Chinese theater in many ways. It is an art form that combines stylized acting with singing, musical dialogue, martial arts and fantastic costumes.

The roles are categorized according to sex, age and disposition. Females roles are called "dan", male roles "sheng" and the clowns "chou". Each is characterized by different patterns of facial make-up. The colors and patterns of these painted faces, called "jing" or "hualian", help the audience distinguish a good character from a cruel or sly one. The costumes and head-dresses are magnificent works of art.

Kunqu Opera

Ancient Chinese poetry is the key to this 500-year-old theatrical show. The cadences of the poems are matched to about 1,000 melodies, from different parts of China. The acting is colorful and the dancing graceful.

Pingju Opera

Originating from a northern Chinese folk ballad art form called "lianhualuo" and folk dances called "bengbengxi", this opera uses colloquial narrative and deals with the everyday life, popular among ordinary Beijingers.

Hebei Bangzi

Accompanied by "bangzi" (wooden clappers), this opera form, native to the region around Tianjin, Beijing and Hebei Province, features passionate singing, tragic stories, fan dances and a unique vocabulary of facial expressions. It is said that a Hebei "bangzi" actor can sing up to 100 sentences without flagging.

Puppet Shows

There has been puppetry in China for 2,000 years and it has developed into a comprehensive art combining drama, song, dance, music, painting and sculpture. China Puppet Show Artistic Troupe is in the lead in this art.

Acrobatics

Chinese acrobats have long been famed for their seemingly impossible contortion and balancing ability. The China Acrobatics Troupe and Beijing Acrobatics Troupe have won many international prizes in Paris, Morocco and other parts of the world for their performances. The two troupes and the acrobatic team of the Railway Performing Troupe give regular shows at the Rehearsal Hall of Beijing Acrobatics Troupe and Chaoyang and Erqi theaters.

Opera

Foreign visitors may be surprised to find that they can watch Madame Butterfly or Carmen in Beijing. The Central Opera Theater is mainly dedicated to stage Western operas, while the China Opera Theater performs the Chinese operas with a mixed singing method of Italian bel canto and traditional Chinese singing.

Symphony

Founded in 1951, the Central Philharmonic Orchestra is one of the few orchestra which can offer the repertoire from George F. Handel to Peter Tchalkovsky. The orchestra performs symphony concerts in Beijing Concert Hall every week. In addition, Beijing Philharmonic Orchestra is a rising star in the field of Western music.

Song and Dance

Some national-class troupes in Beijing perform music and dance from various parts of China. They are the Central Song and Dance Ensemble, the Army's Ensemble, the Oriental Song and Dance Troupe, the Beijing Song and Dance Troupe, the Central Nationalities Song and Dance Troupe who are composed of artists from different ethnic groups, and the Central Nationalities Orchestra.

Among them the Oriental Song and Dance Troupe is noted for its performances adapted from countries around the world. Overseas visitors are impressed by the Royal Song and Dance performed by Beijing Song and Dance Troupe.

Ballet

The Central Ballet Troupe is the only ballet troupe in Beijing. It has the best ballet artists and symphony orchestra in China.

Drama

As an alien art form, modern drama has a history of 70 years in China. One of the renowned theaters, Beijing People's Art Theater, offers a wide repertoire of Chinese dramas adapted from ancient stories and foreign plays by world-class playwrights. Drama amateurs flood to the Capital Theater, home stage of the People's Theater, to watch Lao She's Teahouse, Bernard Shaw's Major Barbara and Caine's Mutiny by Herman Wouk.

SPORTS

Long distance running is a traditional sport in Beijing, which has held a Spring Festival Round-City Race for the past 21 years. The city also hosts marathons—including a world-class one recognized by the International Amateur Athletic Federation.

International and national sports competitions are usually held in spring and autumn. The important venues are the National Olympic Center, where the Asian Games was held, and the Worker's Stadium in eastern suburban region.

Other favorite sport events for Beijingers include table tennis, volleyball, badminton, swimming, martial arts, and, of course, soccer.

TENNIS

Beijing International
Tennis Center
50 Tiantan Donglu
9:00-22:00
Tel : 7013872

Olympic Tennis Center
Asian Games Village
Tel : 4912233 ext 327

GOLF

Beijing International Golf
Club

Beijing Golf Club

Changping County
Tel : 9746388

Shunyi County
Tel : 9441111

Beijing County Golf Club
Shunyi County

SHOOTING

Civil light weapons are available. Special ranges are set up and technical service is provided by qualified personnel.

China North International
Shooting Range
Nankou Town, Changping
County
Tel : 9771368

Great Wall Shooting Range
Huairou Town
Tel : 9643573

HORSE RACINGS

Wissotel Horse Racing
Club
Dongsi Shitiao
Overpass
Tel : 5012288

Beijing Horseman's Park
Beizang Village, Daxing
County
Tel : 9254019

(Offering betting account of Hong Kong Royal Horse Racing Club. Live TV show of house races in Hong Kong and Macao every Wednesday and Saturday in racing reason.)

Rural Horse Racing Range
Mapo, Shunyi County
Tel : 9441499

SWIMMING

Sino-Japanese Youth
Exchange Center
40 Liangmaqiaolu
Tel: 4663311

Ying Dong Swimming Pool
Olympic Sports Center
Tel: 4910483, 4910468

HUNTING

Miyun Hunting Ground
 Yaoxiang Valley, Xinchengzi Township, Minchengzi Township, Miyun County.
 Blessed with picturesque rivers and mountains, the ground boasts various wildlife, such as hare, deer and pheasant. Guide service, guns and bullets can be provided. Hunters are not allowed to bring their own equipment.
 Tel: 9944472
 Primitive Tribes Garden
 Sanduhe Township, Huairou County
 Tel: 9644633
 Horse racing, hunting, fishing and sacrificial performances.

BOWLING

New Century Hotel
Tel: 8492001 ext 35708

Holiday Inn Lido Hotel
Tel: 4376688 ext 3805

China World Hotel
Tel: 5052266 ext 41

Tianlun Dynasty Hotel
Tel: 5138888

ANGLING

Bixi Angling
Garden
Zhangjiachang Village
Fangshan District
Tel : 3814927, 9351120
ext 241

International Angling
Garden
Lishuiqiao Park
Chaoyang District
Tel : 5138933, 4232042

Lantianmei Fishing
Village
Laiguangying Beilu
Chaoyang District

Tel : 4231178

Beichen Jiangzhuang

Lake Fishing Center
North of Asian Games
Village

MARTIAL ARTS (Chinese Kung Fu)

Yuanmingyuan Ruyi Martial Arts School
　　It is the only private martial school approved by the
city government. Attendants may learn various styles of
Chinese boxing and Qigong (a Chinese breathing exercise)
to enhance the physique.
　　152 Yuanmingyuan Lu
　　Tel : 2571596, 2587485

FITNESS CENTERS AND HEALTH SPAS

Lisheng Health Town Club
　　A combination of body-building facilities and enter-
tainment.
　　A1, Yuetan Nanjie (Inside Yuetan Stadium)

Tel : 8511114

Fitness Center of Beijing Dance Academy
19 Minzu Xueyuan Nanlu, Haidian District
Tel : 8412277 ext 245

Chapter 4　BUSINESS IN BEIJING

Stable political environment, rich material and personnel resources, as well as updated infrastructure facilities make Beijing one of the most attractive Chinese cities to foreign investors.

The following is a briefing in commercial possibilities together with a list of organizations devoted to international business.

SERVICE ORGANS FOR FOREIGN INVESTMENT

The service organs offer consultation about establishing enterprises with foreign investment. They help locate investing opportunities and cooperative partners, conducts research on conditions of markets by drafting and revising project proposals, doing feasibility studies, preparing protocols, contracts and other business documents. The Beijing Foreign Enterprise Service Cooperation provides local employees and relevant services.

Details of application formalities and investment procedures are available from these organs, as is information on income tax, preferential treatments to different types of investment, tax refunds, customs duties on imports and special tax exemption, land use fees, and availability of offices and living quarters.

Business Hours

Offices generally open eight to five with a lunch break of one to two hours and from Monday to Friday. The most significant public holiday is the Spring Festival or the Chinese Lunar New Year when most Chinese make holiday for at least four days. They also celebrate their National Day on October 1, the Labor Day on May 1, and to a lesser extent, the Mid-Autumn Festival.

Business Centers

one of the boons for business people in Beijing is the prevalence of hotel business centers. All major hotels and many smaller, locally-managed properties operate them, which often open around the clock. they are staffed with clerks and computers, photo copiers and fax machines (typewriters can be rented for use in guest rooms). Postal and courier services. Audio-visual equipment can also be found in these centers. Rates for service vary among hotels so it is better to check out in advance.

Photocopying & Printing Services

The facilities in the basement of the West Wing Office Tower of the China World Trade Center offer a complete printing service, includng design of business logos and labels, envelope printing, binding, laser typesetting, fax and computer rental.

In addition, almost all advertising companies provide similar services. Business centers in hotels can offer duplicating and simple printng service.

Convention & Exhbition Centers

The Beijing International Convention Center is part

of a sprawling complex of buildings and stadiums which used to make up the 1990 Asian Games Village. Ths center is facilitated to host conferences, exhibitions, trade fairs, art and fashion shows. There are two main halls. The Grand Conference Hall accommodates 2,800 people and the other seats 600. The exhibition section of the center has four principal halls with a total floor space of 5,500 square meters; besides there are 48 smaller state-of-the-art meeting rooms, an auditorium and a special 48-seat conference hall capable of prividing simultaneous translations in six languages.

The China World Trade Center is a conventon and exhibition complex connected to its hotel and office tower. The main convention hall, which incorporates the latest telecommunication equipment, can house 2,000 people for a reception or theater-style performance. In addition, the complex has a banquet hall for up to 1,100 people at a time, and 38 function rooms for meeting among 10 to 380 guests.

The exhibition center occupies two floors, covering a combined space of 7,387 square meters. It offers direct motor vehicle access. This section can be subdivided into a hall of 3,470 square meters with a ceiling of 4.3 meters, a 2,090-square-meter hall with a ceiling of 2.9 meters, and a 1,818-square-meter column-free loading and unloading hall with a 19-meter high clearance.

Call: 5052266.

The China International Exhibition Center, localted in the northeastern part of Beijing in the vicinity of foreign embassies, is one of the largest exhibition facilities in the country, occupying a total area of 170,000 square meters.

Call: 4664433.

The 21st Century Hotel and the Sino-Japanese Youth Exchange Center combine to form large complex of buildings, including a theater, vocational training center, conference hall, research lab, audio-visual production studio and a wedding palace for young couples.

Call: 4663311.

Media Center, jointly erected by CCTV and NHK, is a complex capable of providing services like TV program production, satellite transference, and accommodation. The center is located beside the West Chang'an Avenue, adjacent to CCTV and Yuyuantan Park.

MANAGEMENT AND SERVICE DEPARTMENTS

BEIJING FOREIGN INVESTMENT SERVICE CENTER

The center was established in 1988 by the Beijing Municipal People's Government and affiliated to the Foreign Economic and Trade Commission. It is the city's earliest and most important investor service organ. The Center is also the permanent administrative institution of both the Beijing Municipal Foreign Investment Administrative Committee and the Beijing Association of Enterprises with Foreign Investment.

The Center acts as a bridge between foreign enterprises and the Chinese government to serve investors of both Chinese and foreign businesses. Its goals are to introduce investment opportunities, to provide high quality and efficient services, and to improve the investment environment.

The Center, with offices and representative agencies within the Beijing Municipality, has set up liaison, business development, and legal affairs departments. Its professionals are not only familiar with foreign economic laws and documentation but are also experienced in mediating economic disputes relating to enterprises with foreign investment. The Center, through many years of operation, has acted as a "Window to Beijing", attracting foreign investors and forming a place of exchange for foreign investment enterprises.

Business Scope:

To work in entrustment with both Chinese and foreign investors by introducing investment opportunities and potential business partners: To draft and revise project report and additional commercial documents for Chinese and foreign investors; to assist foreign companies in setting up representative offices in Beijing; to analyze the investment environment, investigate specific investment projects, and provide business information for potential investors. The Foreign Economic and Trade Commission administers the Center's assistance to foreign investment enterprises with any legal formalities in establishing a base in Beijing. The Center maintains personnel files and insurance for Chinese employees of foreign enterprises, obtains visa applications for business abroad, and evaluates job titles for Chinese senior administrators and for all specific field staff. In addition, the Center assists in obtaining offices and residential housing in Beijing; to arrange foreign trade and technical information exchange for Chinese and foreign investors through conferences, discussions and seminars both within China and abroad; to administer the training of personnel in charge of foreign economic relations, examine and approve legal documents of foregn investors, and train Chinese senior administrators in all specific fields in Beijing; to act as a standing legal consultant for business matters, including mediating legal disputes and undertaking special liquidation; to collect information regarding the investment of foreign capital and provide relevant information and legal services; to provide additional services for Chinese and foreign investors if entrusted.

Add: 7th Floor, Test Building, No. 31 Beisanhuan Zhonglu, Haidian District, Beijing

Post Code: 100088

Tel: 2023332 ext 2708, 2702, 2710, 2109

BEIJING INVESTMENT ADVISRY SERVICE CENTER

The Center aims at catering to the China's fast-growing economy, especially to meet demands of foreign investors for information. The organ is jointly set up by the Research Office under Beijing Municipal Government and the Municipal Planning Commission. Functioning as a go-between service medium, the Center provides convenient service to businesspeople from home and abroad.

Scope of business:

to prepare projects and offer investment opportunities for overseas businesspeople; to provide consultative services on China's investment policy, procedures and conditions for establishment of enterprises with foreign investment; to publish promotion material, organize promotion programs and train negotiation personnel; to conduct market analysis and feasibility study; to conduct all necessary procedures on behalf of foreign investors; to undertake other tasks entrusted by domestic and overseas investors and make commercial deals.

The Center is composed of:

Secretarial and Public Relations Department which receives overseas guests and organizes public relation activities, drafts and traslates documents, and manages personnel files of employees in overseas enterprises; administrates executive, financial and statistical affairs.

Information Department is in charge of collecting and analyzing business and investment information, setting up data base; and collecting and providing project information.

Consultation and Promotion Department is responsible for publishing project information, organizing promotion and negotiations, providng information on government decrees, regulations and investment conditons, conducting feasibility study, market research and drafting legal documents.

General Service Department is in charge of fulfilling complete or partial procedures authorzed by relevant departments of the Municipal Government.

Add: 2A Baiwanzhuang Dajie Donglu, Haidian District, Beijing, 100037

Tel: 8315349, 8315343

BEIJING SUB-COUNCIL OF CHINA COUNCIL FOR THE PROMOTION OFINTERNATIONAL TRADE

Also known as Beijing Chamber of Commerce (hereinafter referred to as the Sub-Council), the Sub-Council is an influential non-governmental organization composed of social celebrities, established enterprises and other economic entities in Beijing.

It aims at promoting Beijing's foregn trade, utilizing foreign capital and technologies and conducting various cooperative activities, thus promoting business and economic development between Beijing and other countries and regions the world over.

Business Scope:

1. To establish contacts with foreign chambers of commerce, international economic and trade organizations, industrial and commercial entities, as well as representative offices of foreign enterprises in Beijing; to participate in relevant activities held by above organizations; to organise and co-host international conventions with relevant organs; and to deliver invitation and host visits of foreign economic delegations and celebrities.

To organize Beijing's economic, trade and technical delegations for inspection tours abroad; to host seminars and symposiums of foreign techniques and products.

2. To provide information on trade and economic cooperation; to operate Beijing international economic information network; and to seek trade opportunities and introduce partners for investment and cooperation.

3. To establish contracts with other international and regional exhibition organizers; to organize Beijing trade enterprises to attend foreign exhibition and trade fairs; to host and provide services for foreign countries and regions, including Taiwan, Hong Kong and Macao, and sponsor trade and technical fairs in Beijing.

4. To offer legal consultation services on international trade, investment and technical transfer for domestic and overseas enterprises and organizations; to serve as legal advisors for enterprises; to mediate economic disputes by operating the Beijing Mediation Center of CCPIT; to issue certifcate of original production base and sign and confirm documents and receipts on foreign trade and shipment.

5. To serve as a trade agent entrusted by enterprises, to process formalities on export commodity trademark registration; to undertake feasibility study and evaluation of certain projects; to cooperate with enterprises in trade negotiations, and to provide services on enterprise management, finance and auditing.

6. To manage Beijing World Trade Center with the joint efforts of Beijing's import and export corporations and major industrial and commercial enterprises; to enhance understanding among members of trade centers worldwide; and to exchange economic information and offer other services.

Add: Dongcheng District, Beijing, 100006
Tel: 5125175, 5125165

USEFUL INFORMATION

Departments Handling Foreign Investment
Beijing Municipal Foreign Economic & Trade Commision
Add: 190 Chaoyangmennei Dajie
Tel : 5236688

Beijing Planning Commission
Add: 2A Baiwangzhuang Dajie Donglu
Tel : 8318025

Beijing Municipal Economic Commission
Add: 2 Zhengyi Lu
Tel : 5193340, 5193410

Commercial Commission of Beijing Municipality
Add: 2 Zhengyi Lu
Tel : 5192619

Beijing Municipal Administration Commission
Add: 2 Zhengyi Lu
Tel : 5193243

Beijing Urban & Rural Construction Commission
Add: 3 First Hutong, Nanlishi Lu
Tel : 8522070

Agri-Forestry Office of Beijing Municipality
Add: 3 Taijichang
Tel : 3088579

Beijing City-Planning Bureau
Add: 60 Nanlishi Lu, Xicheng District
Tel : 8522994

Beijing Industry & Commerce Administrative Bureau
Add: 360B Caihuying Dongjie, Fengtai District
Tel: 3469955

Office of Foreign Enterprise Registration
Tel: 3494310

Beijing Finance Bureau
Add: 15 Fucheng Lu, Haidian District
Tel: 7013564

Beijing Municipal Taxation Bureau, Foreign Section
Add: 13 Xinzhong Jie, Gongti Beilu
Tel: 4660568, 4670631

The State Administration of Foreign Exchanges Control,
Beijing Branch
Add: 79 Yuetan Nanjie
Tel: 8572108

Beijing Price Bureau
Add: 6 Jianguomennei Dajie
Tel: 5194416

Beijing Imp. & Exp. Commodity Inspection Bureau
Add: 12 Jianguomenwai Dajie
Tel: 5004860

Beijing Land Administrative Bureau
Add: East Gate of Temple of Heaven Chongwen District
Tel: 7013326

Beijing Municipal Statistical Bureau
Add: 2 Huaibaishu Jie Xuanwu District
Tel: 3012679

Beijing Investment and Information Advisory Service
Center
Add: 2A Baiwanzhuang Dongdajie
Tel: 8315349

Beijing Foreign Investment Service Center
Add: 7F Kai Qi Building
31 Beisanhuan Zhonglu
Tel: 2023332 ext 2707,2704

Entry & Exit
Passport & Visa Department,
Beijing Municipal Government Foreign Affairs Office
Add: 2 Zhengyi Lu
Tel: 5192882

Office of Entry & Exit Control for Chinese Citizens, Bei-
jing Public Security Bureau
Add: 38 Dongjiaominxiang
Tel: 5241440

Foreign Section of Beijing Public Security Bureau
Add: 85 Beichizi Dajie
Tel: 5255486

Beijing Foreign Affairs & Consultation Centre
Add: 190 Chaoyangmennei Dajie
Tel: 5257829, 5137210

Telecommunication Service
Beijing Telephone Bureau Dongdan Office
Add: 65 Jianguomennei Dajie
Tel: 5124559

Xidan Office
Add: 131 Xidan Beidajie
Tel : 6021511

Business Office of Beijing Long-distance Telephone
Bureau
Add: 97 Fuxingmennei Dajie
Tel : 6022969

Business Office of Beijing Wireless Communication Bureau
Add: 56 Houbanbidian Jie Xizhimennei
Tel : 6050311, 6011333

Beijing International Post Office
Add: Jianguomen Beidajie
Tel : 5128120

Transportation Service
Capital Airport Information
Tel : 4563604

Ticket Office of Civil Aviation
Add: 15 Xichang'an Jie
Tel : 6017755

Reservations for Domestic Flights
Tel : 6013336

Reservations for International Flights
Tel : 6016667

Foreign Enterprise Air Service Corp.
Add: China World Trade Center
Tel : 5053330

Ticket Reservation:
Tel : 5052258, 5052259

Train Information
Tel : 5633622

Beijing Taxi Administration
Tel : 6012620

China Civil Aviation Passenger & Cargo Sales Corp.
Add: 8 Dongxing Road, Sanlitun
Tel : 4665370, 4665371

Fortune Express International Co. , Ltd.
Add: 1 Huanggufen, XiaoguanAndingmenwai
Tel : 4260886 ext 889, 811

China Air Service
Add: 225 Chaowai Dajie
Tel : 5065533

Sinotrans Beijing Company
Seafreight: 4652354
Railfreight: 3814440 ext 211
Air Cargo: 5011014
Exhibition Transportation : 4671713
Automobile service: 3813378

Banks & Finance
Bank of China, Beijing Branch
Add: 19 Dong'anmen Dajie
Tel : 5199416

The People's Bank of China, Beijing Branch
Add: 9 Xiheyan, Qianmen

Tel : 3035254, 5199437

State Administration of Exchange Control
Beijing Branch, Regulatory Center
Add: 79 Yuetan Nanjie
Tel : 8572106

The Industrial & Commercial Bank of China, Beijing
Branch
Add: 10 Baiyun Lu
Tel : 3013101

The People's Construction Bank of China, Beijing Branch
Add: 1 Maliandao Beilu, Guanganmenwai
Tel : 3265301

The Agricultural Bank of China, Beijing Branch
Add: 15 Shuidaozi Hutong
East gate of Temple of Heaven
Tel : 7014233

Bank of Communications, Beijing Branch
Add: 12 Tiantan Dongli Beiqu
Chongwen District
Tel : 7016528, 7016529

CITIC Industrial Bank
Add: 6 Xinyuan Nanlu
Tel : 5122233

Legal Service
Beijing Justice Bureau
Add: 199 Haihutun, Yongdingmenwai Fengtai District
Tel : 7212227

Beijing Notarial Office
Add: Building 25, Jishikou Xiaoqu
Chaowai Dajie
Tel : 5077112

Beijing Foreign Economy Law Office
Add: Working People's Cultural Palace
Tel : 5133167, 5133168

Beijing Tian Ping Law Office
Add: 20 Wangfujing Dajie
Tel : 5135261

China Global Law Office
Add: 3F SAS Royal Hotel
6A Beisanhuan Donglu
Tel : 4652315

China Legal Consultancy Center
Add: Rm 418, Television Service Building
20 Wangfujing Dajie
Tel : 5135261

Express Mail & Moving Service
DHI-Sinotrans Ltd.
Add: 45 Xinyuan Jie
Chaoyang District
Tel : 4662211

HPS
Add: 12 Anding Lu
Tel : 4651565

EMS
Add: 7 Qianmen Dongdajie

Tel : 5129947, 5129948

TNT
Add: Building 14, Shuguang Xili
Tel : 4677877 (Delivery)
     4672517 (Inquiry)

Beijing Shuang Chen Express Co. Ltd.
Add: 9 Nongzhanguan Nanlu
Tel : 5084775, 5067719

Crown Pacific (China) Ltd.
Add: Rm. 1104, CITIC Building
Tel : 5002255 ext 1140

Office Buildings
China World Tower
Add: 1 Jianguomenwai Dajie
Tel : 5052288

Jingguang Centre
Add: Hujialou, Chaoyang District
Tel : 5013388

Lufthansa Centre
Add: 50 Lianmaqiao Lu
Tel : 4663388

CITIC Bulding
Add: 19 Jianguomenwai Dajie
Tel : 5002255

Capital Mansion
Add: 6 Xinyuan Nanlu
Tel : 4660088

SCITE Tower
Add: 22 Jianguomenwai Dajie
Tel: 5122288

Asia Pacific Building
Add: 8 Yabao Lu, Chaoyang District
Tel: 5139988

Fortune Building
Add: 5 Dongsanhuan Beilu
Tel: 5018811

Hui Bin Mansion
Add: 8 Beichan Donglu
Tel: 4993886

Xing Fu Mansion
Add: 3 Dongsanhuan Beilu
Tel: 4615760

Exhibition & Convention Centers
China International Exhibition Center
Add: 6 Beisanhuan Donglu Chaoyang District
Tel: 4664433

China World Trade Center Exhibition Hall
Add: 1 Jianguomenwa Dajie
Tel: 5053832

Beijing International Convention Center
Add: Asian Games Village
Tel: 4993571

Beijing PICO Exhibition Services Co. Ltd.
Add: Rm. 401, Building 8, Hua Qiao Apartment, Anhuili

Area 3
Tel : 4916592

Beijing Exhibition Center
Add: 135 Xizhimenwai Dajie
Tel : 8323551

Beijing Media Center
Add: 11B Fuxing Lu
Tel : 8514422

Sino-Japan Youth Exchange Center
Add: 40 Liangmaqiao Lu
Tel : 4663311

APPENDIX

USEFUL EXPRESSIONS

Hello!	Ni hao!
How are you?	Ni hao ma?
Very well, thank you.	Hen hao, xie xie.
Good	Hao
Very good, very well	Hen Hao
Not good	Bu hao
Bad	Huai
Good-bye	Zaijian
I am sorry/excuse me	Dui bu qi
I don't know	Wo bu zhi dao
Do you understand?	Ni ting dong le ma?
I don't understand	Wo ting bu dong
Please wait a moment	Qing deng yi deng
It doesn't matter	Mei you guan xi
You are welcome	Bu ke qi
Please tell me...	Qing wen...

Pronouns

I	Wo
We	Women
You	Ni
You (plural)	Nimen
He, she, it	Ta
They	Tamen

Transport

Taxi	Chuzuche
Bus	Gonggong qiche
Trolley bus	Wugui dianche
Minibus taxi	"Miandi"
Bicycle	Zixingche
Railway station	Huochezhan
Airport	Jichang
Where to?	Qu naer?
Where is Beijing Hotel?	Beijing fandian zai naer?
Hotel	Lüguan/fandian/binguan
Park	Gongyuan

Shopping

Go shopping	Qu mai dongxi
How much?	Duo shao qian?
Do you have...	You mei you...?
I want...	Wo yao...
Don't want	Bu yao
Too expensive	Tai gui le
A cheaper one	Pian yi dian de
US dollar	Meiyuan
RMB	Renminbi

Numbers

0	Ling
1	Yi
2	Er
3	San
4	Si
5	Wu
6	Liu
7	Qi
8	Ba
9	Jiu
10	Shi
20	Ershi
100	Yibai
200	Lianbai
300	Sanbai
1000	Yiqian
10000	Yiwan
20000	Lianwan

Dining

Restaurant	Canting/fandian/fanguan
Delicious	Hao chi
I have had enough	Wo bao le
Too much/too many	Tai duo le
Cheers	Sui yi
Bottoms up	Gan bei
To your health	Zhu nin jian kang
Toilet	Ce suo

Geographical Terms

East	Dong
West	Xi

North	Bei
south	Nan
Middle	Zhong
Street	Jie
Avenue	Dajie
Road	Lu
Alley, lane	Hutong
District	Qu
County	Xian
Gate/door	Men
Outside	Wai
Inside	Nei

Business

No problem	Mei wen ti
Just a moment	Deng yi xia
It doesn't matter	Mei you guan xi
I want...	Wo yao...
How much?	Duo shao?
Toilet	Cesuo
Airport	Jichang
Train station	Huochezhan
Hospital	Yi yuan
Stop here	Ting zher
Hotel	Fan dian
Telephone	Dian hua
Miss	Xiao jie
Mr.	Xian sheng
China World Trade Center	Guo mao zhong xin
Friendship Store	You yi shang dian

Editor: Ai Shan
Translated by: Song Zhenfeng
Designed by: Han Fengze
Final reading by: Huang Junqing and Liu Zongren

BEIJING GUIDE

Published by China Today Press
(24 Baiwanzhuang Road, Beijing, China
Postcode: 100037)
Distributed by China International
Books Trading Corporation 35 Chegongzhuang Xilu
(P.O. Box 399, Beijing, China.
Postcode: 100044)
Printed by Foreign Languages Printing House
First edition: 1996
17 – CE – 3065P
ISBN7 – 5072 – 0847 – 8/Z·190
03200